JUJITSU
BASIC TECHNIQUES
OF THE GENTLE ART

EXPANDED EDITION

GEORGE KIRBY

JUJITSU
BASIC TECHNIQUES OF THE GENTLE ART
EXPANDED EDITION
GEORGE KIRBY

Edited by Sarah Dzida,
Wendy Levine and Jeannine Santiago

Graphic Design by John Bodine

©2011 Cruz Bay Publishing, Inc.
All Rights Reserved
Printed in the United States of America
Library of Congress Control Number: 2011922724
ISBN-10: 0-89750-198-5
ISBN-13: 978-0-89750-198-9

Fourth Printing 2018

BLACK BELT BOOKS
A Division of **OHARA** 🅘 **PUBLICATIONS, INC.**
World Leader in Martial Arts Publications

TABLE OF CONTENTS

INTRODUCTION (1983)

Jujitsu is the "gentle art" of self-defense. It is an ancient art that unfortunately received little notice until the last quarter of the 20th century. This is because of a number of related factors. There are few instructors who are qualified to teach jujitsu in the United States as compared to the other more popular martial arts of judo, karate and *aikido*. Most jujitsu instructors also teach through local YMCAs or parks because they choose to teach for the enjoyment (as their *sensei* did) rather than at a private *dojo* where finances and livelihoods can become a concern.

There have also been very few definitive writings on the art in contrast with the other martial arts. This book will attempt to shed some light on the art of jujitsu by defining the art, presenting its history and philosophy, and giving instructional guidelines that will help the serious student develop his knowledge. This book also will present a number of techniques that will start the student on his way toward perfecting the art as a means of effective self-defense. Upon satisfactorily perfecting the techniques presented in this book, a student will be about halfway through the purple belt (fourth *kyu*), according to the standards of the American Jujitsu Association, an internationally recognized governing body of jujitsu in the United States. AJA tests have been included at the back of this book for handy reference.

This book could not have been possible without the time given by two jujitsu professors in training me over the years. I'd like to take this opportunity to express my sincere gratitude to Jack Sanzo Seki, *hachidan*, jujitsu, for taking me under his wing in the 1960s and providing me with the opportunity to learn and teach the art under his careful guidance. Gratitude also must be extended to Harold T. Brosious, *rokudan*, *ketsugo* jujitsu, who showed me another facet of the art. Without these two giving people this book would not be possible. Additional thanks also must be given to my wife, Adel, who was patient with me during the process of writing this book, Kevin Harte, *nidan*, and Robert Harte, *shodan*, who gave their time to help shoot the pictures, and the staff of Ohara Publications, who worked very closely with me to perfect this book for your education and enlightenment.

—George Kirby
January 1983

Photo by Thomas Sanders

INTRODUCTION (2011)

Wow! It's been almost 30 years since I originally wrote *Jujitsu: Basic Techniques of the Gentle Art*. Since its release in 1983, a lot of things have happened.

First, the book has served as a basic resource for a multitude of martial arts instructors and students inside and outside the traditional *jujitsu* community. It is used as a basic self-defense text by colleges around the United States. Instructors in other martial arts use it as a core reference to broaden their students' martial arts backgrounds, as well as explain basic martial arts theories and concepts.

Second, I've gotten older, a bit heavier, a bit slower physically but hopefully a bit wiser. As someone once said, "The fortitude of old age and stealth will win over youth and exuberance every time." I don't think it's stealth as much as patience and a greater understanding of the art. I've found that jujitsu, as all other traditional arts, continues to be viable even though my needs and abilities change. Thanks to keeping myself flexible, I can still do most of the jujitsu techniques I did in the 1960s, although some of them are far more refined now. Remember, practice, practice, practice, or good old *kime-no-kata* (practice the form without executing the technique).

Third, I've seen some martial arts crazes and well-publicized martial artists secure the limelight only to disappear several years later. However, *Jujitsu: Basic Techniques of the Gentle Art* has remained a bestseller. It has been reprinted virtually unchanged over the years, and this is perhaps its greatest asset. It set the standard and continues to be a standard for serious instructional martial arts books.

So why update it? Why tinker with something that's working? These are legitimate questions that deserve to be answered. My reasoning is that things have changed. The techniques are still credible and are still taught as they were almost 30 years ago, but some of the wording in the techniques has been rephrased for greater clarity and understanding. I've also updated the basic "sensitive points on the human body" chart to be more in line with the techniques presented in this book. The chart also indicates the potential level of injury at each point. This is done to help students develop an understanding of the importance of self-control in executing any technique to these particular body parts. Pain is relative; injury is absolute!

Also, there have been some structural changes in the belt-rank requirements over the years to help assure a higher level of student success. These include the addition of an attitude element, cross-referencing techniques among instructional sequences and various book and DVD resources, and the addition of Japanese names to all the techniques. I've also added a detailed history of the formation of *budoshin* jujitsu and an explanation on how the inclusions of *bujutsu*, *bugei* and *bunkai* are important elements of the art. These changes ensure that students will develop a greater quantitative and qualitative knowledge of the art. By the time students test for black belt, their level of technical knowledge will be higher than when *Jujitsu: Basic Techniques of the Gentle Art* was first published. Their understanding of the art and how it works also will be vastly improved.

There is a real difference between a black belt or *sensei* who can simply do techniques and defend himself well at the drop of a hat and one who can do that plus explain the operational theory behind any particular technique in an intelligent and coherent manner. After all, students will ask questions, and they deserve competent, knowledgeable and coherent answers and physical examples. *Jujitsu: Basic Techniques of the Gentle Art* now will help potential black belts reach that level of competency.

Last, I have acquired additional historical information over the past several years to more firmly establish budoshin jujitsu among the traditional martial arts. Numerous people in governmental agencies and martial arts organizations in the United States and Japan unselfishly assisted me in this part of my martial arts quest.

These additional changes have occurred because any competent teacher will always seek out ways to increase student competence, proficiency and success at every level of learning, as well as seek to garner information from primary sources whenever possible. A conscientious teacher also will learn a lot about teaching from his students—including better teaching methods—if he creates a positive learning environment because those students are the beneficiaries of his guidance. As a public-school teacher and martial arts instructor, I have gotten some of my best and most successful teaching ideas from my students. The subject matter and content may be the same at all levels of proficiency, but ultimately, the level of competence is improved. This concept also applies to the reconfigured belt-rank exams in the revised section of this book.

In summary, the intent of this updated edition is to provide you with information and materials that are being used by me today and not 30 years ago. The subject matter is essentially the same. Improved technique explanations should help you learn the techniques faster. The techniques presented in this book still will get you up through the fifth or blue-belt level and part way into the fourth or purple belt, just like in the original book. The technical requirements have not been increased. Students will, however, develop a better understanding of the art.

So, as I conclude this update, what other "wisdom" can I convey? First, I am honored to have been asked to update my first book. I had no idea that writing the first book would start me on a journey I am still traveling. In the process, I've met a lot of terrific people and learned even more about jujitsu. Thank you for your continued support, which has made this possible.

Second, learning a single martial art is a lifelong process. If you have an open mind—and challenging students—there is always more to learn. I will probably be a student of the art for the remaining years of my life. I have accepted that status. The new things old sensei learn ultimately help them and their students become better practitioners of the art. So, if you're serious about your martial art, take the time to learn and understand it even if it takes your entire life. As my sensei Jack Sanzo Seki once said, "When you start out in a martial art, you are a white belt. When you achieve certain skill levels, you are a white belt. When you die, you are a white belt—because you are still learning the art." The white belt eventually becomes black only because of the time, effort and experience the wearer puts into practicing the art.

Third, I have learned that my students are an invaluable resource and are more than willing to help improve the instructional program. Whether it be a new way to teach a difficult technique so that students can learn it within five minutes, employing computer or other technical expertise, revising belt requirements, cross-referencing sources or serving as *uke* in my books, students who help improve the learning of the art have been recognized and are mentioned in this book. I firmly believe that if someone provides that special help, then recognition should be given. I would not have been able to accomplish all that I have without the help of many tremendously giving people.

Finally, and most important, when you have become a black belt or sensei in the martial arts or at any other skill, do not keep your knowledge to yourself. If you do not help others, you have not truly learned the art. You don't truly learn how to do something until you teach someone else to practice that skill or art at least as well as you do. Become a sensei and a resource for others. You have an obligation to "pay it forward" and help others on the path up the mountain.

—George Kirby
January 2011

CHAPTER 1
JUJITSU: THE GENTLE ART

History of Jujitsu

*J*ujitsu has not had a neat, organized history as many other martial arts have. It is easier to trace a martial art when there is a single source from which it began. It is more difficult to trace the roots that form the base of an art. Such has been the case with jujitsu.

The practice of jujitsu can be traced back in history more than 2,500 years. Jujitsu (*ju* means gentle; *jitsu* means art) developed from many individual teachings that either originated in Japan or found their way to Japan from other Asian countries. In 2674 B.C., the first mention of martial arts comes from Huang-Di (China) who founded *wu-su* (martial arts), a concept in which the body was used for self-defense purposes. Going far back into Japanese legend, you might be able to trace jujitsu to the ancient Japanese gods Kajima and Kadori, who allegedly used the art to chastise the lawless inhabitants of an eastern province.

The first dated mention of jujitsu occurred between 772 and 481 B.C., when open-hand techniques were used during the Choon Chu era in China. In A.D. 525, Bodhidharma, a Zen Buddhist monk, traveled from India to China, visiting the Shaolin monastery. He soon combined Chinese *kempo* (*kenpo* in Japanese) with yoga breathing to form Shaolin *chuan fa* (*shorinji kenpo*[1] in Japanese). As legend has it, Bodhidharma eventually developed the system further into what became *go-shin-jutsu-karate* (self-defense art of open hand). In 230 B.C., the wrestling sport of *chikura kurabe* developed in Japan and was integrated into jujitsu training. Approximately 2,000 years ago, there is also mention of the development of wrestling and related techniques that served as the base of jujitsu.

There is evidence that empty-hand techniques were in use during the Heian period (794-1185) in Japan, but they were used in conjunction with weapons training for samurai. In 880, Prince Teijun (also known as Sadagami) formed the Daito-ryu Aiki Ju-Jutsu School. *Daito-ryu aiki jujutsu* was based on the secret teachings of *shugendo* (*shu* means search, *ken* means power, *do* means way), the eventual source of *kendo*, which uses circular hand motions to assist in defending oneself with weapons. It was from this school that Morihei Uyeshiba took portions of the art to start his own system of *aikido* in 1925.

---

[1] *Shorinji* is the Japanese spelling of the Chinese word Shaolin. The Shaolin monastery is considered to be the source of *sil lum kung fu*.

Most of the credit for founding the formal art of jujitsu goes to Hisamori Tenenuchi, who formed the first school of jujitsu in Japan in 1532. In 1559, Chin Gen Pinh, a monk, migrated from China to Japan, bringing kempo with him, parts of which were integrated into the current teachings of jujitsu. During the Tokugawa era (circa 1650), jujitsu continued to flourish as a part of samurai training.

The next historical phase of jujitsu, which had gone into decline with the closing of the Tokugawa era, was in 1882, when Jigoro Kano developed the sport of judo from jujitsu in order to increase the popularity of the martial arts and to provide a safe sport using selected techniques taken from the art of jujitsu.

Jujitsu in the West

Jujitsu made its way to the United States in the early 20th century. Although there are historical accounts that indicate President Theodore Roosevelt practiced jujitsu, it actually may have been judo. The significant influx of the art was first felt in Hawaii and on the Pacific Coast of the United States in the period from 1920 to 1940, during which time a number of Japanese migrated from Japan. A second influx was felt following World War II when a number of U.S. military men returned from tours of duty in Japan.

There is no single style of jujitsu in the United States today. This is perhaps a weakness. Jujitsu has been called many things in the United States, from one form of karate to a synonym for judo. This may be a consequence of Americans' desire for simplification or their ignorance of what jujitsu really is and where it came from.

Regardless of the style of jujitsu, practitioners all seem to cover the same material. Even though there may be different emphases and elements may be taught in different sequences, the art has survived. This is its strength. It has been flexible enough to endure through the ages and grow once again in today's world.

Budoshin Jujitsu

Jujitsu: Basic Techniques of the Gentle Art is based on the teachings of Jack Sanzo Seki, aka Jack Haywood, who began offering his instruction to the public in the early 1960s. Seki was a traditionalist who believed that there were no styles, or *ryu*, of jujitsu. He believed that once you got past terminology (in English and Japanese) and variations in the execution of specific techniques, it was all the same. It is for this reason that I have added Seki's Japanese terminology to all the techniques in the updated revision of this book. These are the terms Seki used, even if they were very generic names. Many of these techniques may have different names in different ryu of the art. It makes for a Pandora's box any way you look at it. Seki may have used generic terminology to simplify it for his students. It also may have been his way of having his students think of techniques in categories, based on the general technique used or the body part used/attacked rather than as unrelated individual techniques. This is why identical Japanese names are sometimes used for similar techniques. Seki's terminology is used throughout this book because that is how Seki taught the art.

As Seki taught all the jujitsu techniques as responses to realistic street attacks, even for white belts, all the techniques presented in this book follow the same concept of effective self-defense. Jujitsu as taught by Seki is tremendously effective and efficient; many of his former students, including myself, have found this out in real street situations. A proficient practitioner can cause great pain with no injury or devastating injuries designed to completely immobilize a physical attacker. Seki also stressed the need for calmness and control in street situations. Although Seki was not physically abusive, he did push many students to the brink of their tempers or beyond just to test their mettle. He lost many students in the process. However, he believed that it was his responsibility to weed out students who couldn't control their feelings. According to Seki, if you're going to have students learn devastating self-defense techniques, they also must have the self-control and common sense to know where and when to use them.

Jujitsu Defined

Stated simply, jujitsu[2] is the "gentle art" of self-defense. This is a very simple definition for a very complicated art. It does have a more complex definition. If we look at the many characteristics of the art, it will be possible to come up with a more complete definition, one that is more suitable for the serious student.

First, jujitsu is what might be called a "parent art." A parent art is an art from which other martial arts develop. Because jujitsu has such a broad history, it was inevitable that other arts, or more correctly, "ways" would evolve from it. Judo ("gentle way") and aikido (the way of mind and spirit) can trace direct lines to jujitsu. Many styles of karate, especially kenpo, also can trace some of their techniques back to jujitsu. Therefore, in addition to being a parent art, jujitsu is also a combination of many of the more popular martial arts taught today. On observing a practitioner of jujitsu, you will see flashes of each separate do. You will also see how many separate moves can be combined into an effective self-defense system.

Jujitsu is a series or combination of techniques that have been separated

---

[2] *Jujitsu* also can be spelled *jiu-jitsu*, *jujutsu* and any number of hyphenated ways, but they all refer to the same art.

into other arts. Why was jujitsu separated into specific do or ways? Jujitsu may have become too complex as an art or, because there was no single system or systemized way of teaching it, too difficult to learn. Kano and Uyeshiba were able to simplify and systemize their ways. There are perhaps 30 to 50 basic moves in jujitsu. However, it is the combinations and variations of the basic moves that make the art so complex and almost infinite in its variety. By dividing the art into three general areas (judo for throws and leverage, karate for strikes and hits, and aikido for nerves and the use of attacker momentum), portions of the art became easier to teach. They were also easier to organize and perpetuate as a system.

As they become easier (a relative term) to teach, organize and perpetuate as a system, the "way" became more attractive to potential students. I am not placing a value judgment on the validity of any martial art because all arts are effective when placed in their proper context. I am merely presenting one logical possibility in the evolution of the martial arts. Jujitsu was in decline in 19th-century Japan, a time period when other martial arts were rising in popularity. Jujitsu was a complex art. The other martial arts were also complex, but because they could be organized and limited in their scope, they became easier to teach. Their growth was inevitable.

Jujitsu ultimately survived by traveling two parallel pathways. There were those who continued to teach it as a traditional martial art, realizing that students would recognize the virtue of studying jujitsu and pass that knowledge on. There were also those who studied one of the do that evolved from jujitsu, became proficient, realized something was missing and developed proficiency in each of the other do that make up a major portion of jujitsu. In their own way, they put the pieces of the puzzle back together again. It may not have been quite the same puzzle that jujitsu started out as, but all the pieces still fit. They were able to integrate judo, karate and aikido back into the martial art of jujitsu to provide an effective system. This perhaps is where some of the more modern terms, such as *karate-jitsu*, *aiki-jitsu* and combat judo come from.

This theory of two paths can be borne out by observing the variety of styles of jujitsu that exist in the United States and throughout the world today. Despite their differences in terminology (and sequence in which techniques are taught), they are all remarkably similar. Many, in fact, are identical by the time the student gets to the level of *shodan*. As stated before, it was Seki's belief that there are no *styles* of jujitsu—only the art of jujitsu. History and observation seem to bear that out.

Jujitsu is an extremely effective self-defense system. If jujitsu is taught as an art, the student will have a vast resource to draw on in order to defend himself. He has learned a series of basic moves that can be combined in an almost unlimited manner. His only limitation is his knowledge and understanding of the moves and how and why they work. A skilled student can create and control the amount of pain his assailant may feel without an injury taking place. He also can create sufficient pain and disabling injuries that will make it impossible for the assailant to continue his attack.

If you give a man a fish, he has enough food for a day. If you teach him how to fish, he has enough food for a lifetime.[3] The same theory applies to the martial arts. If a student learns specific defenses for specific attacks, he may survive those attacks. But if he learns a variety of moves as an art, he will survive the attacks and will develop a greater variety of responses to any given situation. He has been given the tools of survival rather than one simple meal.

If jujitsu is taught as an art, a proficient student can use his knowledge to create new and different combinations of moves based on the basic moves he has learned. That is how this book is organized. The student is encouraged to take the basic moves and combinations in this book and my other books, master them and reorganize them into other combinations. It will be like lighting the first candle in a tunnel. You'll be surprised how far you can go.

Jujitsu is also a form of relaxation. There is nothing more rejuvenating than letting your developed *ki* (energy) and *mushin* (state of "no mind") control your situation on the mat. You don't know what attacks are coming at you, and you don't have time to think about them anyway. It's a pleasure to let your ki and mushin control your body, executing techniques smoothly, without your sensing any mental or physical output taking place. This is a skill that is acquired after much practice and patience. This is also what makes jujitsu an art.

A Philosophy of Jujitsu

If a person seriously studies any martial art, it is inevitable that such a study will include the development of a philosophical background. It is also inevitable that as a person grows further into the art, the interrelationship between the physical and mental aspects of the art also will be developed and strengthened. The result can be a philosophy of life in which the martial arts training serves as a base.

Such is the case with jujitsu. There is a philosophy that goes with the knowledge. There is a close interrelationship between the physical and mental aspects of the art, and the resultant philosophy can have a profound influence on one's daily life.

There are a number of factors that affect a student's philosophical growth

---

[3] Anonymous saying.

in jujitsu. The first factor is the physically destructive potential of jujitsu. A skilled *jujitsuka* can control his attacker's ki, which is the inner spirit, driving force or center of energy. If a person commits himself to a course of action, he is committing his ki; his ki is directed toward that end. The skilled jujitsuka can control that energy. As a student becomes more knowledgeable in the use of nerves and pressure points, he will also develop the ability to create and control pain without doing any real harm to his assailant. Combine both these elements with the ability to create real pain and disabling injuries, and you can recognize the potential control and havoc that a skilled student can deliver to an attacker.

Because of this destructive potential, jujitsu places a strong emphasis on the concept of nonviolence. A physical confrontation should be avoided whenever possible. There are two additional reasons that support this concept of nonviolence. First, as the jujitsu student becomes confident of his skill, he recognizes that he has a better-than-average chance of defending himself successfully. Thus, it is unnecessary to prove it if such a confrontation can be avoided. Second, a physical confrontation indicates that all rational means of resolving the problem have failed. It is humanly degrading to become involved in a physical confrontation because it indicates that reason and intelligence have failed.

A second factor that will affect philosophical growth is the knowledge that can be obtained by studying the art. In addition to learning the forms and moves of the art, there is also the continuous process of combining and varying the forms to deal with the same or different situations in different ways. It is an infinite mental process. Once the student masters basic techniques and the ability to integrate them, the result is greater confidence.

The student's ability to control his *own* ki and an attacker's ki is a third element affecting growth. To control his own ki the student must be relaxed. Learned techniques should flow from the center of the body automatically, spontaneously. The student can sense and use his attacker's ki only if he (the student) is relaxed. If the student can control his ki, it is possible for him to remain calm and in control of himself in stressful situations.

Fourth, an understanding of the circle theory can be of profound importance. At this point, the circle theory will be stated simply: Everything moves in a circular motion. For every action there is an appropriate consequence suitable to the action. This theory, with respect to the physical aspect of the art, will be dealt with later in greater detail.

The last major factor affecting the philosophical growth of the student is the circumstances under which the art is learned. If the student is taught jujitsu solely as a means of self-defense, then that is all the student will learn.

If the student learns jujitsu as an art, perhaps for relaxation as I did, he can gain much more. He can look at the art as an art form rather than solely as a means of self-defense. He can see *why* techniques are done as they are and what makes them work. Rather than just learning techniques, he can learn to *understand* them. If he can understand them, he can adapt them to different situations and integrate basic moves with one another, knowing in advance what the consequences will be. The process can be related directly to daily life.

The philosophy of jujitsu as an art is based on the concept of continuity. Within the teachings of jujitsu, there is the concept of the continuous flow of things: By extending your own ki, you can control the ki of others, and by controlling the other person's ki, it is possible to control that person. While techniques must be modified to meet different situations so must you be able to change to meet new situations successfully.

Learning the art also involves developing a great deal of patience. Techniques cannot be learned and then put aside. They must be constantly reviewed, improved on, modified and perfected. A good instructor will strive to train his students psychologically as well as physically, like my sensei did with me. "Words are cheap," Seki would always say. The higher in rank we became the more verbal harassment we had to put up with in class. The harassment served to encourage those of us who stuck it out to do better. It also taught us not to let words affect us, who we were or our goals. To persist in our studies was our goal. Patience was the key.

By understanding jujitsu—the *art* and its concepts—it is possible to recognize that you can have greater control of your environment while accepting it at the same time. By studying the art, you can develop a better understanding of the limits of your environment, yourself and others. This is particularly true if you, too, become a sensei. Students will come to you as clay, each one with a different malleability. You can do a great deal with your students if you nurture, mold and push them. You can help them recognize their own potential.

With time and training, a student will develop a feeling of self-confidence combined with humbleness and not feel it necessary to always prove himself. He can be patient, tolerant and understanding of others—a real asset to growth. He will also develop greater self-control, recognizing that he can control his environment through confidence and an understanding of his abilities. All this can give the serious student a positive outlook on life. Jujitsu can be learned as an art in all its facets. It can give the student an understanding of what life is and how to be an active participant in it.[4]

---

[4] For more information about philosophical elements go to page 131.

Photo by Thomas Sanders

CHAPTER 2
TECHNICAL PRINCIPLES OF JUJITSU

In order to develop jujitsu as an effective means of self-defense, there are a number of skills that must be acquired and developed. These can be placed into two general areas: ki development and the actual mechanics of techniques. If you practice techniques and moves regularly, your proficiency will be developed and improved. It is essential that you take your time while learning. Rushing will get you nowhere fast. Patience and persistent practice, directed toward perfecting techniques, will bring you the confidence that accompanies success.

Ki Development

Ki development is one of the two most important factors in making jujitsu techniques effective for self-defense. It is one thing to go through the mechanical moves of each form, but it is quite another to execute them without any apparent mental or physical effort. Ki development will help make that possible.

What is ki? It is considered to be the source of power or energy in the human body, the cause of momentum when the human body directs itself toward a goal. Metaphysical tradition holds that your ki is located approximately one to two inches below the navel at the hypogastrium or *saiki tanden* (lower stomach). That is where the center of your energy or center of gravity is located. It is the focal point for many jujitsu techniques.

Ki is also energy directed from the body. This concept is especially true in aikido and the many *te waza* (hand techniques) of jujitsu. In using these techniques, the student directs his ki through his body and out through his fingertips in order to execute what appear to be effortless defenses against an attacker while not actually grabbing the attacker's arm or hand to execute one of many responses (a release, hold, takedown, throw or come-along).

This is a difficult concept to explain. As my instructor explained it to his students, ki is like an electrical field. In order to use ki effectively, it is necessary that the hand and fingers be relatively straight and relaxed so that they can direct the energy in the direction the fingers are pointed. If the fingers are bent with the fingertips facing your palm or your fist is tightly clenched, it is impossible to extend ki because it is redirected back into your body.

The same concept can be applied to all jujitsu techniques. You should always look in the direction you are going—never at your attacker—while executing a technique. If your techniques are executed properly, there always will be a flow of ki in the direction you are looking or where your fingers are directed.

Ki development requires that you be relaxed mentally and physically.

Only under these conditions will your mind and body be at ease and receptive to your ki. You must be in a relaxed state to operate most efficiently. By being relaxed, you also can sense your attacker's ki and use it to your advantage. With a calm, clear mind and relaxed body, you can more readily react to (or anticipate) unforeseen changes and be able to direct your body accordingly with very little or even no apparent conscious thought taking place. Admittedly, this is not the easiest thing to do in a street situation, but it can be done if the student is proficient in his knowledge and practices on a regular basis.

Ki development also requires that you learn how to use your attacker's strength, which is concentrated in *his* ki. When attacking, your opponent will use muscle (that is, strength) to accomplish his goals. In the process, he will create momentum and a direction of force. Recognizing that the attacker's strength will usually be greater than yours, it is essential that you use *his* strength, not yours. If you are calm and relaxed, it will be easier for you to accept and use his ki, *helping* him to reach his goal. In other words, you will redirect his ki or enhance it with your own to bring your attacker down in the direction he was directing his ki. It is possible, and often necessary, to use your ki to maintain control of the attacker and the situation.

Excitement, nervous anticipation and tenseness are your worst enemies. Any of them can cause your body to release large quantities of adrenaline, a hormone that enhances body strength during times of great stress. If you can remain relaxed, you can control the adrenaline flow. If you cannot control its flow, you may lose control of your body and your ki.

Jujitsu techniques will only work if you are calm and in control of your body. Calmness is reflected in your ability to keep presence of mind in an otherwise tense situation—even though you are aware of what is happening or has happened and feel scared. If you remain calm, keep your presence of mind, speak in a low voice and refrain from indications of fright, you have a better chance of getting out of the situation successfully.

Smoothness in the execution of techniques will come with time, practice and experience. Jujitsu techniques operate best when done smoothly—one motion flowing into another—without any choppiness. Choppy executions will provide the attacker with the chance to regain control of his ki when your ki is not flowing smoothly. You will be successful when you can execute techniques without any apparent effort.

The key is not trying at all. Sometimes the harder you try to do something, the more difficult the task becomes and the more elusive the goal. If you are relaxed and calm, you have a greater chance of success. If you are relaxed, your ki will do your work for you.

Speed cannot compensate for a lack of development in the aforementioned factors. Speed is a consequence that will come naturally as proficiency in techniques increases. Proficiency *and* speed are required for effective self-defense techniques. However, speed cannot compensate for a lack of proficiency.

It is also necessary to master the techniques you use for controlling the potential damage that can result to your attacker. Most states have laws that frown on the use of excessive force. Though I am not an attorney, I believe that it can be safely stated that no one will deny you the right to defend yourself. It is what you do in the process of defending yourself that may cause problems. Effective self-defense does not mean beating your opponent to a pulp. Self-control means doing only what is necessary to protect yourself so you can remove yourself from the immediate environment.

Another essential aspect to the development of ki is your *kiai* (literally, "spirit meeting"), more commonly referred to as a loud, aggressive yell. There are numerous reasons for developing a good kiai. Practically, a kiai draws attention to your situation. Secondly, it should scare and intimidate your attacker. Lastly, a good kiai makes it possible for you to completely extend your ki to control the attacker's ki when the situation warrants.

One last element in the development of ki must be explained. That element is flexibility. You and your techniques must be able to change as the situation changes. A person grabbing you may not warrant the same response like someone who is trying to hit you. Yet the first may be a prelude to the second. Anticipation can be a friend or foe. If you anticipate what is going to happen, it is possible to plan for it. However, anticipation also may tunnel your preparations toward only one attack or direction. Flexibility can avert this negative consequence of anticipation.

Flexibility also allows you to smoothly move from one technique to another. Such flexibility is acquired after techniques are learned well and the mechanics of their operation are understood. It is this area that will be dealt with next.

Ki development covers many areas: relaxation, strength, calmness and smoothness, speed, control, kiai and flexibility. All are interrelated and dependent on one another. Ki development is essential for the proper execution of techniques. In jujitsu, ki is the key to success.

Mechanics of Techniques[5]

Jujitsu techniques are relatively easy to learn if you approach them with an open and positive mind. If you also understand the mechanics behind the

---

[5] Much of this material is quoted directly from my article "The Artful Transition From Empty Hand to Weapons" (*Black Belt*, December 1981).

techniques, they are easier to understand and learn. For this reason, some time will be spent in this chapter covering some of the general mechanics of the art before moving on to specific techniques.

All the techniques in this book are taught right-handed. This makes it much easier for the majority of people to learn initially. If you are left-handed (as I am), be patient and learn the techniques right-handed. It will be no more difficult for you than a right-handed person. Once you've learned everything right-handed, you should then learn the techniques left-handed by simply doing everything the opposite way. At this point, a left-handed person will usually have a distinct advantage because he has superior coordination on his left side.

All the techniques in this book also require that the defender start all moves from a right ready position *(tachi waza)*. This will allow you to start from a balanced position. Most of the techniques in this book are inter-changeable. A technique used for a lapel grab also can be used for a hit, club attack, choke, etc., with only slight modifications in the initial reaction to the attack.

The use of strikes and nerves form an integral part of jujitsu techniques, either to loosen up an opponent as part of an actual technique or as a finish to a technique once the opponent is on the ground. Nerves and pressure points are those points in the human body, usually at a body joint, where nerve centers can be attacked. The attack may be a simple application of pressure by one finger. This may result in controlled pain (with no injury), loss of blood circulation or a stunning feeling identical to an electric shock resulting in a muscle spasm, numbness or muscle contraction, which can be used to loosen up an attacker. The use of simple pressure also makes it possible to control and redirect the attacker's ki.

A nerve or pressure-point attack also can be in the form of a hit or kick. In this case, the amount of force is not as important as the speed at impact and how fast the hit or kick can be withdrawn. The strike is supposed to stun, not injure. Almost all hits of this type are done with the open hand. Many successful stunning blows can be dealt with the palm of the hand in a cupped position. Again, the intent is to stun, not injure.

The ability of the jujitsu practitioner to develop the use of nerves to create pain is based on his ability to become proficient in the use of empty-hand techniques combined with an understanding of ki and the circle theory of movement. By acquiring a good understanding of empty-hand techniques, the student also will acquire an understanding of ki and the circle theory.

When attacking, an attacker commits his ki to the direction of his attack. He is extending his center of energy in that direction.

When attacked, use your ki to stop his force and counter it directly, as in Figure 1. Your ki also can be used to absorb the attacker's ki and either continue his direction of force or redirect his energy in another *complementary* direction, as in Figure 2.

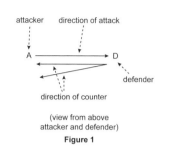

attacker   direction of attack

A ————————→ D

defender

direction of counter

(view from above
attacker and defender)

Figure 1

Attacker momentum is the end result of the attacker's extension of his ki. It is that amount of energy that is directed toward a certain point (Figure 3). The momentum, as an expression of his ki, is what is used by a jujitsuka as a basis for his response to the attack. It is the ability to sense and use the attacker's momentum that makes circle-theory techniques possible.

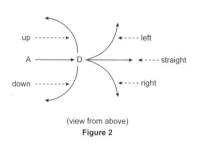

up - - - - - - →

left

A ————→ D ←————→   ←- - - - straight

down - - - - - - →

right

(view from above)
Figure 2

The circle theory is a very simple and extremely complicated concept that deals with the movement of the attacker. The basic idea is this: Through the use of the attacker's ki, momentum, nerves and pressure points, and the use of your own ki, you are able to direct the attacker in any number of directions by extending his ki in a circular motion. To accomplish this, the defender must become the center of the circle with his extremities serving as the spokes that radiate out to the edge of the circle. Figure 4 gives a basic idea of the circle theory. If an attacker (A) strikes at you with a hit or a club, you move out of the direct line of the attack, deflect the hit and then continue its direction in a circular motion, bringing the attacker down. The movement of the defender in directing the attacker's ki must *encourage* the circular motion. Even though the attacker may not make it beyond the ground (G), the motion and the ki must be extended beyond that point to guarantee success.

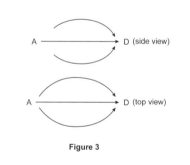

A ————————→ D (side view)

A ————————→ D (top view)

Figure 3

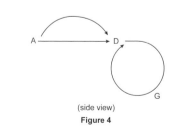

A ————————→ D

G

(side view)
Figure 4

The circle theory also allows movement to the left or right (Figures 5 and 6); up to the right or left for a kick (Figure 7); or, if against a knife thrust or swipe (Figure 8, a double circle one to block the wrist and the other to execute the throw. The application and combination of circle-theory movements are limited only by the defender's skill and knowledge of techniques and the attacker's ability to survive them (attackers rarely survive the defense).

You may have noticed that the moves illustrated in Figures 5 to 8 all involve changing the direction of the attacker's momentum. This is accomplished by redirecting the attacker's ki in a complementary direction. A complementary direction is one that is usually less than 90 degrees to the right or left, up or down, from the direction of the attack. The change in direction is usually a circular motion incorporated into the circle that actually results in the throw (Figure 9).

The chart on page 29 indicates sensitive points on the human body that can be attacked in a number of ways, either as a nerve attack or as a strike. If you choose to strike some of these areas for purposes of delivering a powerful blow, it is best to

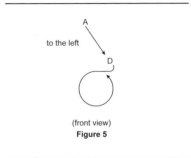

(front view)
Figure 5

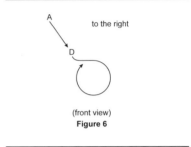

(front view)
Figure 6

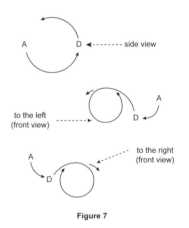

side view

to the left
(front view)

to the right
(front view)

Figure 7

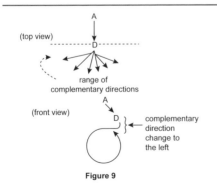

(top view)

range of
complementary directions

(front view)

complementary
direction
change to
the left

Figure 9

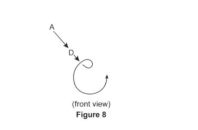

(front view)
Figure 8

use your elbow or kneecap. Either of these parts of the human body will allow you to deliver the greatest amount of force within a given area. You should be aware that any striking technique can cause severe injury, often internally, which can permanently damage your assailant, in addition to causing a great deal of pain and discomfort.

Vital Attack Areas on the Human Body

The diagram shows some of the vulnerable points on the human body. Some of these points can be most effectively attacked with a *gingitzu* or *shuto* strike. Other points are better targeted with a push by the middle finger while the other fingers act as a support. Still other points can be more effectively attacked with a slight pinch.

☐ Slight damage (moderate or sharp pain)

☐ Slight to Moderate damage (may numb or stun for short periods – possible injuries)

■ Slight to Serious damage (possible serious or permanent injury or fatality)

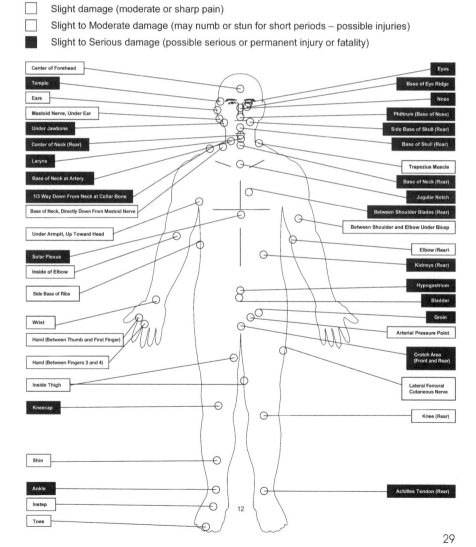

29

You and Your Partner in Practice

Learning jujitsu as an effective art and as a means of self-defense requires a great deal of practice. However, once learned, it is extremely effective and very easy to do. Jujitsu techniques are only useful if they are automatic reactions. It is impossible to effectively learn jujitsu without a partner. You must work with another human body to get the feel of the techniques. All jujitsu techniques are taught as reactions to street attacks. There are no formal *kata*, as in karate.

The study of jujitsu requires two people who are willing to work together and trust one another. Basic to this willingness and trust is the requirement of caution and courtesy. If you are the attacker, you must realize that your partner is learning techniques. Your attacks need not be overly aggressive. Align them with the proficiency of your partner. As you each become more proficient, you can become more aggressive—within reason. In this way, you can help each other increase your skill and self-confidence.

As the person executing jujitsu techniques, you must be considerate of your attacker. Jujitsu techniques are designed to cause injury, usually breaking or dislocating an extremity at a joint. Linear, "green branch", or torque fractures are a common result. (These fractures go up or down the length of a bone and are usually caused by excessive torque applied to the extremity.) Execute techniques slowly at first, gaining proficiency with each move. Starting slowly also will allow your attacking partner to move in the direction you wish, thus reducing the chance of injury. As you become more proficient in your techniques and your partner becomes more proficient in his ability to follow your techniques, you can increase the efficiency and speed of the techniques you are practicing.

It is never wise to resist jujitsu techniques. Resistance can result in serious injury quite easily. Jujitsu is based on ki and leverage, not strength. All your partner may have to do is exert an ounce or two more effort, and you will end up with a sprain or fracture. There is a rule you can follow to protect yourself when you're being thrown: *go with the throw*. If you can't or you're being submitted and the hold is set or starting to hurt, you should immediately indicate submission by calling *maitta* ("I submit") or by tapping your partner or the mat until the hold is released. Don't try to see how much pain you can take or for how long you can take it. Subtle injury may take place that can have long-range cumulative consequences. Be cautious and courteous.

As the *uke* (person to whom the technique is being applied), it is also extremely important that you not get ahead of the movements of the *tori* (person executing the technique) with the hope that by doing so you will be better protecting yourself. There are two major reasons for this: one for the benefit of the tori and one for the benefit of the uke.

The tori needs to learn how the techniques feel when they're executed properly. If the uke moves ahead of the movements of the tori, the tori can't really "learn" the technique beyond going through the movements of it. The uke has to follow the lead of the tori so that the tori can feel what the proper execution of the specific technique feels like.

The uke should follow the guided movements of the tori for safety reasons. Do not get ahead of the movements of the tori. If the tori decides to change direction or even the technique, your committed momentum as the uke will make it impossible for you to change your direction and you may be seriously injured as a result. Also, you need to know what the technique feels like when it's being executed. This knowledge will help you when you switch from being the uke to the tori because you will have a better understanding of how the technique is actually working.

Proper clothing and a proper workout area are essential for safety. A single-weight *judogi* is strongly recommended as the proper uniform. A judogi will take the stress of jujitsu techniques without the risk of tearing. Because a judogi can take a lot of abuse, students can be more aggressive with their learning; they don't have to worry about their opponent's clothing. They also tend to be roomier than karate *gi,* thus simulating regular clothing better.

This has a very important street application. In a street situation, you cannot worry about you or your attacker's clothing. Your concern is protecting your body. If you're worried about clothing, you'll never be able to defend yourself. Using a judogi helps dispel this concern. There is nothing more psychologically damaging to an attacker than finding himself thrown to the ground, possibly injured, and seeing his clothes in shreds. That's supposed to happen. One of the aspects of successfully defending yourself is to create psychological fear in your opponent regardless of the amount of physical damage you have done to his body.

The second advantage of a judogi is that it is fairly loosefitting. This will allow you to move more freely while practicing techniques. Admittedly, you wouldn't walk around the street wearing a judogi. However, the intent is to learn techniques correctly, and street clothes will hinder some moves or tear if you complete those moves. This doesn't mean that the technique is a poor one. It means that your clothes are preventing you from moving. What's important is that you're protecting your body.

Your workout area is equally important. A good minimum area is about 150 square feet of mat space. You could even use a mat area of 8-by-8 feet, as I did, if you are careful about where you are when you throw your uke and where he will land. If you have to practice in this 64-square-feet mat space, you *will* learn where your uke ends up, simply for the sake of safety. It's also valuable for street situations because where an attacker lands can be just as important as how hard he lands. Do not use "exercise" mats because they don't provide adequate impact absorption. Don't use foam mattress pads because your feet will sink down in them, which is a very serious safety hazard for you and your partner. They also will not provide the impact absorption necessary for your uke. Good mats are necessary for your own and your partner's protection. Without them, it is impossible to learn techniques effectively and it will be difficult to avoid serious injury.

You and your partner must assume a learning attitude on the mat. You must be willing to help each other learn the techniques correctly. This requires verbal and physical communication. As beginners, you should cooperate with each other completely, learning how to do the techniques correctly. As you progress, you can become more assertive. However, you must accept the fact that when a hold is set correctly, you need to go in the direction the tori wants you to go for your own protection. To do otherwise is to invite serious injury. On the other hand, you shouldn't fall or go down for your partner just to make him happy. If you are truly friends who are sincere in your desire to learn and help each other, you will help each other learn to do it right.

CHAPTER 3
PREPARATIONS

Before we study the basic techniques illustrated in this text, it is necessary to cover a few basic principles and examples of falling and landing properly. No one gets hurt falling. Gravity controls which direction you will fall—usually down. However, it is important to know how to land—how to hit the ground with proper breakfalls, spreading the shock out over your torso and extremities—to reduce your chances of injury. The importance of learning how to land properly cannot be overemphasized, as many martial artists of experience can tell you. Your *dojo* training will require you to take many falls, over and over again, especially in the art of jujitsu. So this is a skill you should practice regularly so that your breakfalls are automatic, just like your jujitsu techniques need to be.

Knowing how to fall and land instinctively may be invaluable to you in a street confrontation. If you are caught unaware and thrown off-balance, you will be able to absorb the shock of a fall on concrete or other hard surfaces and significantly reduce your chances of injury. This enables you to defend yourself further or run away from danger if you can. Although the knowledge and proficiency in proper falling and landing techniques are essential in reducing your chances of injury, it would be incorrect to say that you will never be injured. However, in a worst-case scenario, a broken wrist or arm is a far better injury compared to a skull or hip fracture.

READY POSITION
Tachi Waza

(A) The right ready position is a relaxed stance with your left hand ready to block (hand open and fingers together) and your right hand clenched in a fist and ready to strike, if necessary. You may raise both hands higher than shown if you want to protect your head and upper torso better. You also may keep your hands open, with your palms facing the attacker. This open-hand position also allows you to adequately defend yourself while creating the visual impression that you don't want to have a physical altercation, which you don't. The right foot is pointed about 45 degrees to the right of the direction you are facing. You should be able to look down and see the front half of both feet. The left ready position (B) is the exact opposite, with your right foot forward. Your body should be relaxed so you can move quickly and more easily.

BASIC SIDE FALL
Yoko Ukemi

(1) Start from a squatting position with your left foot out. (2) Let your body fall backward to the left side; don't jump. Strike the mat with your entire left arm, palm down, and the left side of your left leg as your hips hit the mat. Your arm should be about 45 degrees from your body. Do not reach out or back with your arm to break the fall, though this is a normal reaction; reaching for the ground can cause an injury to your wrist, elbow, or shoulder, or it can cause a fracture. (3) You should land on your left side with your legs apart and your head off the mat. Yell loudly *(kiai)* just before you hit the mat to force the air out of your lungs.

(If you don't get the air out of your lungs before you hit, it will get knocked out of you anyway. If you lose your breath, you can't respond and get back up until you are breathing again.) (1A) As you get more proficient, you can work up to doing the side fall from a standing position. (2A) Be prepared to hit hard with your left arm and kiai to absorb the shock of hitting the ground. (3A) Your left arm should be angled about 45 degrees from your body for proper shock absorption. NOTE: You should practice all falls for both the left and right sides. Insert "right" into the above directions to execute falls on the right side.

BASIC BACK ROLL/FALL

Ushiro Ukemi

(1) Start from a squatting position. Tuck your chin in. (2) Fall back, using both arms to break the fall. Both arms should slap the mat at about 45 degrees from your body. (3) Tucking your head to your left, roll over your right shoulder (4) onto your right knee (5) and then back up into a ready position. As you get more advanced, you should try this from a standing position. Be sure to tuck your head in to your chest and break the fall with both arms. Do *not* reach back to break a back roll.

BASIC FORWARD ROLL
Mae Ukemi

(1) Squat down, placing your right hand in front of your left hand. (Both hands should be turned inward slightly.) Tuck your head to your left and (2-4) push off with both feet, rolling up your right arm onto your right shoulder and then down diagonally across your back to

your left buttock. (5) As your legs fall forward, break your fall (or forward momentum) with your left arm by slapping the mat. This will help absorb the shock and train your reflexes to slap the mat every time you are on the receiving end of a practice throw.

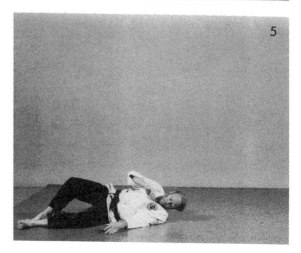

BASIC FORWARD FALL
Mae Ukemi

(1) As you get more proficient at the forward roll, work toward doing the fall from a standing position. (2) Make sure your hand is always palm down, whether or not it touches the ground. (Keeping it palm down lines up your arm and body muscles properly for a safer roll.) Remember to tuck your chin in toward the opposite shoulder of the arm you're using to guide your fall. In this sequence, you're guiding with your right hand. Therefore, tuck your head to

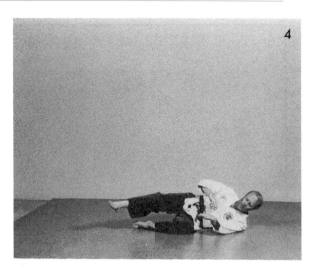

your left. (3) Break your fall as your body is about to hit the mat. (4) You should then tuck your left knee under your right leg, (5) raise yourself up onto your left knee (6) and get back up in a ready position, turning at the same time to face your attacker. Avoid using your hands as you get more proficient because you will need your forearms to block any incoming kicks or hits while you are down. If you're using your hands to get up, they can't protect you.

CHAPTER 4
BASIC TECHNIQUES

Jujitsu, unlike arts that solely emphasize kata, is an art that must be learned through contact. You need to train with another person so that you can develop the feel for what is required to execute a technique correctly and for how a correctly executed technique feels. You need to know how another human body reacts to what you are doing. For this, constant training with others is the only way to understand jujitsu and its usefulness. Keep in mind that some techniques will be more difficult to learn than others and that none can be mastered overnight.

The majority of the sequences that follow combine two techniques: First, there is a response (for instance, a block) to a specific attack, followed by a control technique or submission (such as a joint lock). The control techniques may be combined with different responses, and therein lies the almost infinite combinations found in jujitsu. Refer to the chart on page 126, and you will see the many different techniques that may be used to respond to specific attacks. Experiment with various combinations, and you will discover how vast this art can be.

One book cannot possibly demonstrate all the techniques of jujitsu, but the sequences here will acquaint you with the most basic ones. This book is best used in conjunction with personal instruction.

BASIC ONE-ARM HIP THROW

Koshi Nage/Ippon Seoi Nage

Submission:

WRIST-LOCK-LIFT SUBMISSION

Tekubi Shimi Waza

(1) Your attacker grabs your clothing with his right hand. (2) Grab his right sleeve with your left hand and (3) strike his solar plexus with your right fist as you move toward him. (4) Step to the inside of your attacker's right foot with your right foot. Your right arm goes under his right arm. (5) Pivot to your left on the ball of your right foot as you bring your left foot back. Both your feet should be inside his feet. (The heels of your feet should be closer together than the front of your feet, but they shouldn't touch.) Squat straight down so that your waist is below his waist and his right thigh is resting between your buttocks. Hold your opponent tight against your back. (6) Lift your opponent off the ground by straightening your legs and bending over at the waist. Let your leg muscles do the work, not your back. Throw the attacker by turning to your left and looking to your left. Do not look at your attacker. Be sure your right hip is blocking his right hip. (7) Once your attacker is down, drop down onto your right knee and (8) bend his right arm down by slipping your left hand down to the back of his wrist and slipping your right arm under his arm, grabbing your left forearm. (9) Your left knee pushes down on the side of your opponent's head as you straighten up your torso, which pulls up on the back of his bent wrist. If done quickly, the wrist will snap.

Technique:
BASIC DROP THROW
Tai-Otoshi

Submission:
WRIST-PRESS
KNEE-DROP SUBMISSION
Tekubi Shimi Waza/Shioku Waza

(1) Assume a ready position as your attacker is about to strike. (2) Block his punch away to your left with your left forearm, then (3) slide your left hand down to grab your attacker's sleeve, stepping across with your left foot. (4) Pivot counterclockwise (to your left) on the ball of your left foot as your right hand grabs your attacker's clothing on his right shoulder. (5) Lift your right forearm to strike your attacker under the jaw as your right foot blocks his right leg below his knee, as close to his ankle as possible. Your right knee should be bent slightly against his right leg, with your right foot lined up right next to the outside of his right foot. Ideally, your right big toe should be tight next to his right little toe. This will guarantee that he is blocked low at his ankle. Before executing the throw, be sure you are balanced. This is initially done by looking directly forward and down. If you can see your left kneecap and the front of your left foot directly below it, you should be well-balanced for the throw. As you develop a feel for the throw, this will no longer be necessary. (6) Straighten your right leg sharply as you pull with your left hand and push with your right, turning to your left (all at the same time). Be sure to keep your entire body in a straight line from your right foot to your shoulders. (7) Once your opponent is down, slide your left hand so that your left thumb is on the back of his right hand and your fingers are underneath. (8) Bring your right thumb and fingers next to your left hand to grab his wrist as you drop down on his biceps (optional move) with your left kneecap for the submission. Dropping fast can break his wrist.

LEG LIFT
Ashi Ushiro Nage

Submission:

GROIN STOMP
Kinteki Tatake

(1) Your attacker grabs you from behind, pinning your arms with a bear hug. (2) Bring your leg up and (3) stomp down on his instep with your heel, causing him to relax his grip. (4) Shift your right leg to the outside of his right leg. As you step back slightly with your right leg, your butt will strike the attacker's torso, which further off-balances him. At the same time, it will be easier to bend over quickly to grab his right leg just above his ankle. (5) Lift his leg up to your right thigh, throwing him off-balance. (6) Be sure that you stop his foot at the upper part of your right thigh and not the middle of your groin. (7) Stomp down with the heel of your left foot into the attacker's groin or any area below his belly button.

Technique:
DROP THROW
Tai-Otoshi

Submission:
CHEEKBONE STRIKE
Kao Tatake

(1) Your attacker sets a rear forearm choke with his right arm and pulls you so that your back is slightly arched. Have your left leg forward. (2) Strike your attacker hard in his lower left ribs with your left elbow. Then reach up with your right hand and (3) grab his right shoulder. Grab his right elbow (or sleeve) with your left hand. (4) Hold tight and drop straight down onto your right knee. Your right kneecap should be just in front of his right foot so that his right leg is blocked. (5) Turn to your left as you drop, causing your opponent to be thrown over your right shoulder. (6) Keep hold of his right sleeve or wrist and (7) strike his right cheekbone with your right palm.

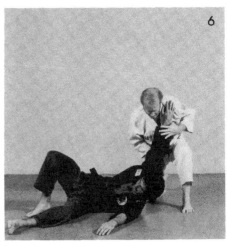

THROAT (TRACHEA) ATTACK

Nodo Shioku Waza

(1) You are attacked with a two-handed front choke. (2) Bring your right hand up and extend your fingertips until they rest on your attacker's trachea just below his larynx. (See inset 2A for detail.) (3) Keeping your fingers straight, thrust against the attacker's trachea and straighten your arm. (Inset 3A shows how your arm moves in comparison to your attacker's original position.) (4) Once your arm is fully extended, keep it fully extended, stepping forward with your right foot to execute the technique. To cause your

opponent to fall backward, direct the force of your fingers slightly upward toward the back of his head. If you want him to go directly down, direct the force of your fingertips downward. In a life-or-death situation, this technique could be used as a strike rather than a press. Striking the trachea and/or larynx at this point can cause the trachea to collapse or go into spasms, suffocating your opponent. CAUTION: Do not practice any hard strikes directly at your fellow practitioner's neck, throat or larynx.

55

Technique:

CHIN OR NOSE TURN WITH HEAD LOCK

Ago/Hana/Atama Maki

Submission:

ELBOW STRIKE

Hiji Tatake

(1) Your attacker sets a head lock with his right arm. (2) Bring your left hand up under your attacker's chin (or, as shown in inset 2A, your middle finger under his nose) and (3) turn his head to his left. (4) Be sure to turn your attacker's head to his left by *pushing*. Do *not* pull it back. (5) As he turns and releases his hold, slip your head out of the head lock. (6) Slide your left hand down and around so that your left forearm is under his chin, placing him in a head lock under your armpit. (7) Strike your opponent's back with your right elbow, just inside his left shoulder blade or ideally at the base of his trapezius muscle for a very debilitating strike. Be sure that your closed fist is facing you as you strike. CAUTION: Do not strike the backbone.

Technique:

BASIC HAND THROW
Te Nage

Submission:

WRIST- OR
ELBOW-SNAP SUBMISSION
Te/Hiji Maki

(1) Assume a ready position as you are threatened with a knife. (2) Pivot your right foot back, thus moving your body out of the way of the straight knife thrust. (Note the arrow indicating movement of the right foot.) After his knife hand has passed your left hand, reach for the wrist of his knife hand from behind. (3) Your left hand grabs the attacker's right hand on top of his wrist—so he can't bend his hand—with your thumb between his third and fourth knuckle on the back of his hand. (See inset 3A.) Both thumbs may be put between his third and fourth knuckles, or you could strike his knife hand with your right kneecap to dislodge the knife. (4) Step forward with your right foot as your right hand strikes the back of his right hand with your thumb still in place. (5) Pivot your left leg back (as indicated by the arrow) in a counterclockwise direction as you push his bent hand with your right hand. (6) Turn his hand in a counterclockwise direction while you continue to pivot your left foot back until you (7) bring your opponent down. (8) For a wrist-snap or elbow-snap submission, place your right instep tight against his right armpit with your foot on the ground and his elbow just below your kneecap. Keep his wrist bent down (and his arm straight) and turn it to the left as you turn to your left. Have your left leg away from the attacker for balance. (9) If the attacker still has the knife, take it away from him before releasing him. For the submission (see inset 9A), place your left thumb next to your right thumb behind his hand. This hold also can be used for the throw.

OUTER-SWEEPING HIP THROW WITH CROSS-BODY ARM TRAP

Harai Goshi

(1) Assume a ready position facing your attacker. (2) Block your attacker's right punch outward with your left forearm, leaning in slightly toward your attacker. (3) Block his left punch outward with your right forearm. Slide your left hand down and hook onto the attacker's right forearm with your fingers on top and your thumb underneath. (4) Push the attacker's left arm away and down in a clockwise circle with your right forearm. Do not grab his left arm with your right hand at any time. (5) Move his left arm across his chest toward his right side as you step and pivot in for a basic hip throw.

Continued on next page

(6) Grab the attacker at his right shoulder with your right hand. This will trap his left arm across his chest and behind your body. (7) Squat down to set up for a basic hip throw. You should be set so that you can balance on your left foot when the throw is executed. (8) Sweep your right leg back, keeping it straight and making contact on the lower part of the attacker's right shin (9) as you turn your body to the left (as in a hip throw) to sweep your opponent off the ground. As your opponent is thrown, he can pull his left arm out from under his right arm so he can break his fall. If his left arm is still trapped, the opponent will have to slam down with the outside of his left leg to break the momentum of the fall. (10) From this position, you can drop your right knee onto the side of his chest or your left knee to his head.

Technique:

CORKSCREW

Ude Guruma

(1) When you are threatened with a knife, assume a ready position. (2) Execute a cross-block, with your right forearm crossed over your left forearm and hands open (fingers together) or with closed fists for a stronger block. Meet the force of the attack straight on, deflecting the direction of the blow to your right. Step forward as you block and keep your legs bent slightly so they can absorb the shock of the blow. (3) Grab the attacker's arm at his wrist with your right hand, preventing him from moving his hand (and the knife). Your left hand also turns to grab his wrist. This can be done almost simultaneously as you start to bring the attacker's arm down (4) to your right in a clockwise circle, securing your grab with both hands. Your hands should be grabbing his wrist like a baseball bat. (Note the arrows.) (5) Continue winding his arm in the same direction as you step in under his arm until your right foot is even with the attacker's right foot. (6) Turn your body to your left by pivoting on the balls of your feet so you're facing in the same direction as the attacker. Continue to wind his arm, making a big circle. (7) Continue the wind and pull out and forward to execute the throw. Keep the knife pointed away from your body if the attacker is still holding it. (8) With the throw completed, you may step forward with your right foot, if necessary, to maintain your balance. CAUTION: In practice, be sure to let your partner's wrist slide—don't hold it tight—as you wind his arm. As you're not really twisting his arm with full force, he should execute a forward roll for you out of courtesy so you can get the feel of the technique. Using full force on this technique can cause immediate and serious injury to the shoulder joint or subtle injury that is cumulative over the years.

Technique:

ARMBAR REAR THROW
Ude Guruma Ushiro

Submission:

SHOULDER-LOCK SUBMISSION
Ude Guruma

(1) Assume a ready position as you face an attacker. (2) If your attacker swings with an overhead club, cross-block it in the same manner as the corkscrew technique. (3) Continue to block with your right forearm while your left hand grabs his right wrist and hand. (The first two fingers of your left hand should be on the back of his right hand.) (4) Release the block with your right forearm and use the outer edge of your right hand to strike down on the attacker's elbow to bend it. Bend his hand in at the same time by pushing with your left hand. (5) Move your right arm under his upper arm and clamp your right hand onto the back of his hand. Simultaneously step forward with your right foot. (6) Step forward with your left foot as you bring both your hands straight down, forcing your attacker backward. In a street situation, remain standing as you bring your arms down. CAUTION: Execute this phase slowly and go only as fast as your partner can fall. It is quite possible to tear the shoulder out of its socket. (7) If you choose to do a shoulder-lock submission, drop down with the attacker onto your right knee. Your left hand should rest on the back of his elbow. Push his elbow away from you as you pull his wrist toward you for the submission. NOTE: This is a very traditional way to learn this shoulder lock. There are numerous variations to setting up this very effective lock.

FIGURE-4 ARMBAR WINDING THROW
Ude Guruma Makikomi

ARMBAR SUBMISSION
Ude Guruma

(1) As your attacker grabs you with his left hand and pulls you toward him, lean in slightly (2) so you can more easily and effectively block his hit with your left forearm. (3) Bring your right hand across and deliver a backhand strike (4) to the side or base of his ribs. You may also strike his cheekbone. (See inset 4A.) (5) Move your left hand over the attacker's right arm and then under it, at or slightly above his elbow. Your right hand rests on his right shoulder. Clamp your left hand onto your right forearm, thumb and fingers on top. His right wrist is now trapped in your armpit, and his palm should be up with the outside of his elbow facing down. (6) Raise your left forearm slightly and push down with your right hand to create pain in your attacker's elbow locked in the armbar. (He will go up onto his toes.) (7) Keep pressure against the outside of his elbow with your left forearm as you pivot back on your left foot, throwing him. Exercise caution with your partner here. (8) Bring him down to the ground, keeping hold of the armbar position. (9) For a submission hold, drop down onto your right knee. Make sure the armbar is set tight. Then straighten up your torso and lean back slightly for submission.

OUTER REAR-SWEEPING THROW

Osoto Gari

Submission:

KNEE-DROP BODY STRIKE

Karada Tatake

(1) Assume a ready position facing your opponent. (2) Block his right punch outward and to your left with your left forearm. Step in slightly with your left foot to keep your balance. (3) Move your left foot to the outside of his right foot so that your left foot is parallel to or slightly behind his right foot but pointed opposite from his direction. (4) Your right

hand reaches across and grabs your attacker's left lapel to help push him off-balance as your right leg comes up to sweep his right leg from behind. (5) Sweep his leg up, causing the attacker to fall backward. Be sure to lean forward to protect your own balance. (6) Drop your right knee onto the side of his ribs for a finishing blow.

Technique:

NECK THROW
Kubi Nage

Submission:

SCISSOR-CHOKE SUBMISSION
Hasami

(1) Assume a ready position facing your opponent. (2) Block your attacker's punch outward with your left forearm as you step in with your left foot. (3) Slide your left hand down his arm and grab his sleeve while bringing your right hand up inside his left arm. (4) Strike the side of his neck sharply with your cupped right hand just below the ear (you should hear a "pop" when you hit) and step in with your right foot. The strike will shock the middle ear and cause your opponent a momentary loss of balance. (5) Pivot back on your left foot while you pull your attacker's right arm with your left hand and continue the motion of your right hand, turning to the left, (6) bringing your opponent down. (7) Set a forearm scissor-choke submission by gripping your right arm with your left hand from behind your opponent's neck while your right hand is pressed underneath his left ear. (See inset 7A.) You also may press the nerves behind the trapezius muscle along with the scissor-choke submission to create additional pain. (See inset 7B.)

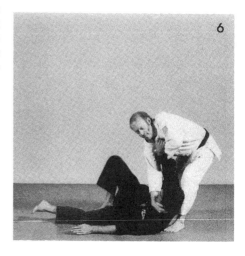

Technique:

INNER-SWEEPING HIP THROW
Hane Goshi

Submission:

KNEE-DROP SUBMISSION
Karada Tatake

(1) Assume a ready position facing your attacker. (2) Block his right punch with your left forearm. (3) Step In close with your right foot, pivoting on your left foot. Your right arm should go underneath his left arm around his body. (This is just one method of grabbing your opponent for a hip throw. Other ways are shown throughout the text. Usually the height and weight of your opponent will determine how you grab him

with your right hand.) (4) Hold the attacker tight against you. Your right foot should be just inside and in front of his right foot. Your right hip does not block his right hip as much as in the basic hip throw. (5) Push your right foot and leg outward against his, to sweep his leg out and up. Continue to move like with a basic hip throw, balancing on your left leg. (6) Once your opponent is thrown, drop your right knee into his armpit for a submission.

Technique:
STOMACH THROW
Tomoe Nage

Submission:
LAPEL CHOKE
Eri Shimi Waza

(1) When your attacker pushes you, (2) grab your attacker's right sleeve with your left hand and his left lapel with your right hand. (3) As you start to fall back, pulling him toward you, place your right foot in the center of his stomach. (4) Roll onto the ground. To execute the throw, push the attacker with your right foot. If you don't want to submit the attacker, let go of his sleeve and lapel as his body passes your head. In practice, keep hold of your partner.

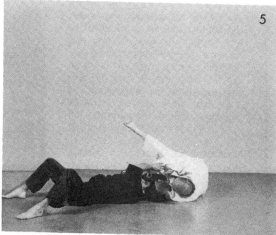

(5) For the submission, keep hold of the attacker and roll over next to him by (6) rolling on your left knee to come up onto your right foot, as shown. Your right hand has brought his left lapel over to the right side of his neck and your right thumb into the nerve of his neck. Pull up with your left hand, automatically setting the choke and nerve attack. (Inset 6A shows where your thumb should be pressing on his neck.)

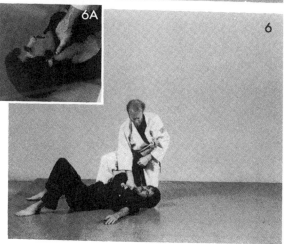

Technique:
FLOATING DROP THROW
Uki Otoshi

Submission:
SHOULDER-LOCK PIN
Senaka Shimi Waza

(1) Assume a ready position facing your attacker. (2) Block his right punch with your left forearm, then (3) step in with your left foot and grab his sleeve with your left hand. (4) Put your right arm around the attacker's head, and kick your right leg to the outside of his right leg as high as it will go. Have your left leg follow your right leg so that you have both feet up in the air, and keep your back tight against the attacker's chest and (for safety's sake) his head tight against you. (5) Turn quickly to your left as you reach your maximum height to bring your opponent over you and down. Make sure your partner gives a *kiai* on this throw. The remaining photographs show the shoulder-lock pin from the opposite side. (6-8) To set a shoulder-lock pin, bring your right leg over the lower part of the attacker's right arm, bending his arm back. (His elbow can be broken at this point if he can't bend his elbow by hooking your right foot under your left knee joint and straightening your left leg.) Maintain the head lock. (9) Once his arm is bent with his palm up, bring your right leg down, turning toward your attacker's head and bringing your left leg up, as shown. (10) Continue this motion, bringing your shin back to your body while you lean forward against his elbow.

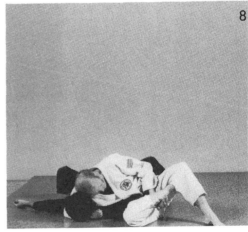

Technique:

FORWARD FINGER THROW

Mae Yubi Nage

Submission:

FINGER BREAK

Yubi Shimi Waza

(1) Your attacker has grabbed your left wrist. Keep your left hand relaxed and open at all times. (This makes it much more difficult for the attacker to sense what you're doing until it's too late for him to do anything about it.) Start to turn *only* your hand, (not your whole arm, and do *not* lift your arm) in a counterclockwise motion (2) over his hand and to your left. Your arm should follow your hand. As your attacker starts to lose his grip, grab his fingers (see inset 2A) with your right hand. (3) Turn to your left on the balls of your feet and bend his fingers back until

he's on his toes. Then push his fingers forward by keeping your wrist locked and applying pressure to the backs of his fingers just below his knuckles. Push outward and slightly upward to execute the throw. (4) Complete the circle by bringing your hand out, down and back. (5) For a submission, drop down onto your right knee, press his palm to the ground and bend his fingers back. NOTE: In practice, grab at least three fingers for this technique. It will give you greater control and reduce the chance of accidentally breaking your partner's fingers.

Technique:
BODY WINDING THROW
Karada Makikomi

Submission:
ARMBAR-TO-SHOULDER-LOCK PIN
Ude Guruma

(1) Assume a ready position facing your attacker. When your attacker starts a sideswipe swing to your head, (2) lean forward to block with your left forearm, stepping forward with your left foot, if necessary, to get your head out of line of his club swing. (3) Your left hand grabs the attacker's sleeve or arm. Turn in (as shown by the arrow) so that you are tight against his body. Thrust your right arm over his right arm, shoving his right shoulder under your right armpit. (4) Block his right leg with your right leg. Lean forward, keeping your entire body straight and turning to your left as you fall. Your right hand may grab onto the attacker's right arm, but it should be done loosely to avoid the chance of injuring your right elbow. (5) When you both hit the ground, be sure your partner says *kiai*. (6) Once you're on the ground, your right arm goes underneath the attacker's right arm and clamps (palm down with your thumb and fingers on top) onto your left forearm, setting a figure-4 armbar. Your right forearm should be just above his elbow. His arm should be palm up. (7) Push down with your left forearm (just above your wrist) on his right arm (just above his wrist) to cause your attacker to release the weapon. NOTE: In practice, if the opponent's arm bends or the outside of his elbow is not facing down, help him bend his arm. Your left hand should then bring his arm down with the back of his hand on the ground, his wrist bent and his palm up. (8) Lean forward, pulling slightly with your left hand as you turn to your left to execute the shoulder lock. Keep your body against his.

LEG-LIFT THROW

Ura Nage

(1) Assume a ready position facing your attacker. (2) As your attacker throws a front snap kick, sidestep to your left with your left foot. At the same time, your right arm blocks outward to deflect the leg and hook it from underneath. (3) After catching your attacker's calf

in the crook of your elbow, step forward with your right leg and reach for the attacker's face with your right hand to execute the throw. (4) Follow through completely by stepping forward with your left leg, if necessary, to retain your balance.

Technique:

INNER REAR-SWEEPING THROW
Ouchi Gari

Submission:

GROIN ATTACK
Kinteki Tatake

(1) Assume a ready position facing your attacker. (2) As your attacker throws a front snap kick, sidestep to your right while leaning to your right to get out of the direct line of his kick. (3) Deflect the blow with your left forearm as you slip your arm under his right leg. (4) Step forward with your left foot and grab the attacker's left shoulder with your right hand. (5) Bring your right leg behind your attacker's left leg and sweep his leg up (6) as you lean forward. Keep your right leg straight as you sweep. (7) Take your right hand off the attacker's right lapel and (7A) strike his groin with your fist, (7B) pull his testicles with your right hand or (7C) drop your right knee onto his groin.

KNUCKLE-PRESS TAKEDOWN

Te Shimi Waza

(1) Assume a ready position facing your attacker. (2) Your attacker grabs your hair with his right hand. (3) Bring both your hands up and grab his hand, with his knuckles in the middle of your palms and your fingers interlocked, trapping his hand on your head. (4) Deliver a front kick with either leg into his groin. (5) Lift his hand off your head, keeping his knuckles squeezed together. (6) Bend his hand back while you push his arm down to

bring the attacker down. Keep your body straight. Do not bend over when you are bringing the attacker down because it will weaken your technique. Bend his hand back more while you either lower your torso (by bending your legs) or take a step back, keeping your body straight, thus creating more pain in his wrist, which will result in greater compliance.

Technique:

WRIST-LOCK-LIFT COME-ALONG

Tekubi Shimi Waza

Submission:

ARM-LOCK COME-ALONG

Tekubi Shimi Waza

(1) When your attacker grabs your hair from behind, (2) grab the attacker's hand with both your hands. (Your thumbs are under his wrist, and your fingers are over his knuckles.) Hold his hand to your head. (3) Pivot your left foot back and turn in to the attacker until you're facing him, keeping his hand trapped against your head. (4) Remove his hand from your head, keeping his wrist twisted and his hand in line with the rest of his arm. (5) Bring the attacker onto his toes by exerting upward pressure at his knuckles. As long as upward pressure can be maintained, your attacker can be controlled. (6) Step around to the back of your attacker and (7) bring his arm behind him, lifting up. (8) As you bring his arm up, bend his wrist, slide your left hand away, and slide your right hand onto the back of his hand with your fingers pointing up and his fingers pointing out. His knuckles should be in the palm of your hand. (9) To set the come-along, make sure that his right elbow is trapped against you. Pull your right hand toward you to exert pressure, create pain and control the attacker. NOTE: This is a proper hold. Resistance to any proper hold causes serious pain and can quite easily result in a fracture or dislocated joint.

NERVE WHEEL THROW

Karada Shioku Waza

(1) Assume a ready position facing your attacker. (2) As your attacker attempts a bear hug, grab his flesh at the side or base of his ribs (each side), thus attacking nerves (see inset 2A) and causing your attacker to release his hold. (Continue turning your hands inward toward his body to cause additional pain. Not only are you digging in deeper with your fingers this way, but the increased pressure of your fingers is

also increasing your control.) Step forward with your right foot toward your attacker. (3-4) Pivot your left foot back, and turn your hands to your left, as if you're turning a steering wheel to your left. The pain you are creating should cause him to leave the ground—to get away from the pain. (5) Once your attacker is on the ground, you can go to a submission. If you try to lift the attacker to do the throw, you're doing it incorrectly.

Technique:

THUMB WINDING THROW

Ube Maki

(1) Your attacker approaches from behind, preparing to choke you. (2) Reach over your shoulder to grab the attacker's thumbs. Grab his thumbs securely (see inset 2A) with your hands, thumbs down. (Grabbing his little fingers is a good second choice.) (3) Lift his hands off and turn to your right. (Inset 3A shows how the attacker's thumbs are held at this stage.) (4) Bring his left arm down across his right arm, at his elbows, thus causing his left elbow to be locked against his right arm. (5) Wind both his thumbs in a large counterclockwise circle, keeping them at opposite points on the "edge" of the circle, to execute the throw. Let go of his thumbs once the attacker is thrown.

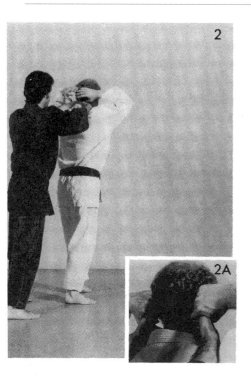

Technique:

SLEEVE PIVOT THROW
Hiki Yoko Nage

(1) Assume a ready position facing your attacker. (2) Your attacker grabs your right wrist and pulls you toward him. Do not resist his pull; you're going to use his strength. (3) Step with your right foot behind the attacker in the direction of his pull, using his pulling force to give you momentum. (4) Grab his right sleeve or arm as you pivot to your left. (5) Pivot your left foot back,

going down on your left knee, and continue pulling his sleeve. (6) When your opponent falls, do not attempt to release your right hand while this technique is being executed. Your hand can be easily turned out once the throw is completed. This throw can be done quite fast and easily if the attacker keeps hold of your right wrist. The throw can still be done if your attacker lets go as long as you've made it to step 4.

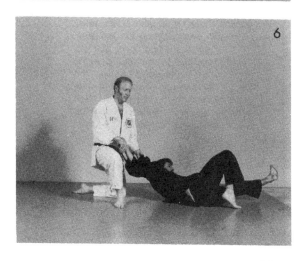

Technique:

WRIST-LOCK TAKEDOWN
Tekubi Shimi Waza

(1) Assume a ready position facing your attacker, who has a knife in his belt. (2) As he draws his knife for a forward thrust, prepare to cross-block. (Your right arm crosses over your left arm midway down both forearms. Your hands are open, but your fingers are together.) Step forward slightly and flex your legs to absorb the shock. (3) Block hard. If done correctly, this will cause your attacker to drop his knife. (4) Your left hand continues to block, while your right hand reaches over your left and grabs his knife hand with your thumb between his first and second knuckles and your fingers under his wrist. Bend his wrist by pushing with your thumb. Start to turn it in a large clockwise circle. (5) As his hand comes up in a clockwise circle, discontinue the block with your left forearm so that your left hand holds the attacker's hand with your thumbs next to each other. (6) Push the knuckles of his hand away from you by pushing with your thumbs while keeping his arm straight by pulling at the base of his hand with your fingers. This small circular motion will cause your opponent to go down. If he moves toward you, take a step away from him and continue the pressure. (7) If he resists the takedown or if you think he might, a good swift kick to the chest or solar plexus will loosen him up. (8) Drop down onto your right knee as he goes down. Keep your back straight. (9) Press his hand toward his body using your thumbs for a submission.

SHOULDER-LOCK REAR TAKEDOWN

Ude Guruma Ushiro

(1) Your attacker shakes your right hand. (What may be perceived as a friendly gesture might actually be a way of preventing you from using your right hand to defend yourself.) (2) Slap your left hand onto the back of his right hand, and grip firmly with your thumb over the top of his wrist and your fingers underneath. (3) Step in with your left foot, and bring his hand up in a counterclockwise circle to your right. (4) As you continue to turn his arm counterclockwise, bring it over your head, pivoting

your body to your right. Your right hand maintains the handshake. (5) Continue turning until you are facing in the opposite direction from your attacker. You should be as close to the attacker as possible during steps 4 and 5 to prevent him from turning out of the technique. His shoulder is now locked. (6) Pull straight down with your left and right hands to take the attacker down. In practice, pull down only as fast as your partner can go down and drop onto your right knee.

Technique:

SHOULDER-LOCK COME-ALONG

Ude Guruma

(1) Your attacker shakes your right hand. (What may be perceived as a friendly gesture might actually be a way of preventing you from using your right hand to defend yourself). (2) Slap your left hand onto the back of his right hand, and grip firmly with your thumb over the top of his wrist and your fingers underneath. (3) Step in with your left foot, and bring his hand up in a counterclockwise circle to your right. (4) As you continue to turn his arm counterclockwise, bring it over your head, pivoting your body to your right. Your right hand maintains the handshake. (5) Continue turning until you are facing in the opposite direction from your attacker. You should be as close to the attacker as possible during steps 4 and 5 to prevent him from turning out of the technique. His shoulder is now locked. (6) Your right hand keeps hold of the handshake. Your left hand lets go of his wrist and grabs his elbow (7-8) as you turn around so you're facing the same direction as the attacker. Pull his elbow to you, thus arching his back. Keep the handshake next to his back. Your left forearm should be resting against the rear base of his skull to provide support for the hold. You can walk the attacker anywhere you want with this hold. Pain is controlled by pulling his arm by his elbow with your left hand.

Technique:

ELBOW-TURN TAKEDOWN
Hiji Waza

(1) Assume a ready position facing your attacker. (2) When your attacker grabs your clothing with both hands, (3) bring your right hand (palm up and slightly cupped) up to your attacker's left elbow. Bring your left hand (palm down) over his right forearm and under his left forearm as close to you as possible. (4) Use your right hand to push his elbow and turn his elbow to your left in a counterclockwise circle as the back of your left hand comes up against the inside of his left forearm. Turn to your left as you raise his elbow. (Inset 4A shows how your fingers point in the direction of the circle.) (5) Continue pivoting. Your left hand turns away from you and grabs the attacker's left forearm (thumb underneath and fingers on top). (6) Continue to roll his elbow, bringing the attacker down. (7) If brought down swiftly, the shoulder will strike the ground first, causing severe injury because of the downward momentum created by rolling his elbow.

Technique:

ARMBAR WINDING THROW

Ude Guruma Makikomi

Submission:

NECK-SCISSOR SUBMISSION

Kubi Hasami

(1) Your attacker grabs your right shoulder from behind with his right hand. (2) Pivot your left foot back and turn to face the attacker. As you turn, bring your left arm up in a counterclockwise circle to your left to protect you in case the attacker attempts a strike with his left hand as you turn. (3-4) Your left arm goes over his right arm and comes up underneath his elbow as your

right hand rests on the attacker's right shoulder. (5) Clamp onto your right forearm with your left hand, thumb and fingers on top. His right wrist should be in your armpit with his palm up and the outside of his elbow facing down. Raise your left forearm up slightly and push down slightly with your right hand to create pain in the attacker's elbow, which should be locked in the armbar.

Continued on next page

(6) Keep pressure against his elbow with your left forearm while you pivot your left foot back, throwing your opponent. (7) Bring him down to the ground. Drop onto your right knee. (8) Set the armbar and neck scissor by pulling the attacker up slightly and bringing your left leg around in front of his neck. (9) Lean back, sliding your right foot under the back of his head.

If you hold the armbar firmly, it will cause his neck to move higher up between your legs. (10) Scissor his neck by interlocking your feet and straightening your legs. (Don't squeeze your legs to choke your opponent. Your leg muscles aren't designed for squeezing. They operate more effectively if you straighten them.) Lean back to execute an armbar submission at the same time.

`Technique:`

HAND WIND ELBOW-ROLL TAKEDOWN

Hiji Waza

(1) Your attacker has his right hand over your mouth and his left hand holding your left arm back. His hand over your mouth is not an effective hold, but it may muffle any screaming you attempt. (2) Loosen up the attacker and distract him by scraping your right heel down his shin and/or (3) stomping down on his right instep with your right heel. (You may even bite or spit on his hand.) (4) Keeping your left hand open and relaxed, turn your hand up and counterclockwise while you pivot to your left. As you bring his arm up, your left thumb should go under his arm so you can grab his wrist. A secure hold is desired, but a tight grip is not essential. (5) Bring your right hand, slightly cupped, up under his elbow and roll (push) it in the same counterclockwise direction. (6) Continue to pivot counterclockwise and push against his elbow. (7) Bring your attacker to the ground. (8) Rest your right kneecap on his upper arm (halfway between his shoulder and elbow) for the submission.

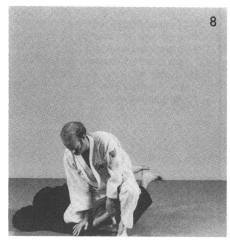

Technique:

HAND WIND ELBOW-ROLL TAKEDOWN

Hiji Waza

(1) Your attacker's right hand grips your right wrist in an arm lock behind your back. (2) Make a fist with your right hand, and use your left hand to grab your right fist. (See inset 2A.) (3) Holding your arm in place in relation to your body, squat down slightly while your left foot sidesteps to your left. Your left hand then pushes down on your right fist as your body moves to the left. Your right foot does not move to the left. This move will put your right arm and hand at your right side rather than behind you, and the attacker's hold can be broken. (4) Let go with your left hand and open up your right hand. Turn your right hand in a clockwise circle to your right as you turn to face your opponent. Your right thumb should be under his wrist so you can grab his wrist. (5) Turn to face your attacker by bringing your left foot around. Cup your left hand and push it up under his elbow. (6) Raise his elbow up in a clockwise direction while turning to your right. NOTE: The left hand is *not* grabbing his elbow. If the palm is kept cupped, it can act as a socket, rotating so that your fingers can point in the direction you wish him to go. (This is using *ki.*) (7) Continue to pivot and push your opponent's elbow to bring him down. (8) Drop down on your left knee. Executing a takedown quickly can result in a serious shoulder injury to your partner.

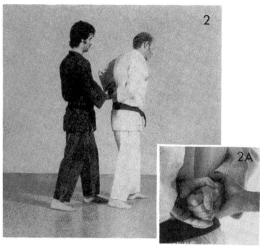

Technique:

ELBOW LIFT

Hiji Waza

(1) Your attacker approaches from behind and (2) grabs your right sleeve with his left hand. (3) Turn to your right toward your attacker, raising your right arm and turning it in a clockwise circle to your right. (4) By stepping toward him, your attacker's arm will bend slightly with your forearm up against the outside of his elbow. (5) Continue the circular movement (keeping your palm facing down), raising his elbow up to get him off-balance. To set a come-along hold, clamp onto your left forearm with your right hand, and raise your right forearm just enough to keep your attacker up on his toes. (See inset 5A.) (6) The upward force of this move causes the attacker to fall backward. (7) Follow through even after the attacker has let go and fallen.

Technique:

HEAD WINDING THROW
Atama Makikomi

(1) Your attacker grabs your clothing. (2) Strike your attacker's solar plexus with your right fist to loosen him up, putting your right shoulder into the punch to maximize the force of the strike. (3) Bring your left hand up around the side of his head, and grab his hair on the opposite side (the left side). To grab the hair properly, your fingers should be spread apart. Slide your hand up around the attacker's head, starting from the base of his head, until your hand is where you want it. Close your hand, grabbing as much hair as close to the skull as possible. This is more painful and gives much better control (as compared to a loose grab of a few hairs) and actually reduces the chance of hair being pulled out because of the larger area affected. (4) Cup your right hand at the base of the attacker's chin. Pull his hair toward you from the left, and push his chin away in a counterclockwise motion to your left. (5) You may need to bring your right foot forward slightly for balance. (6) Pivot your left foot back, and continue turning the attacker's head counterclockwise. Turn it—don't pull it. (7) Bring your opponent down. Drop to your right knee, and (8) quickly turn your opponent's head the other way to snap the neck. CAUTION: This technique is for a life-or-death situation only!

116

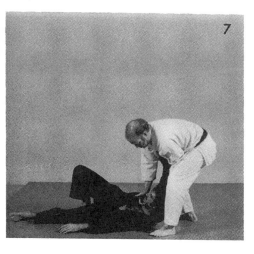

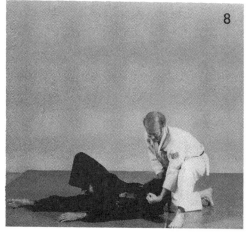

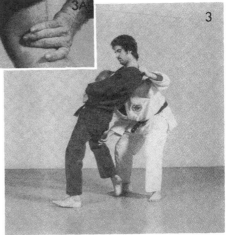

Technique:

REAR LEG-LIFT THROW

Shioku Ashi Ushiro Nage

(1) Your attacker has you in a head lock, using his right arm. (2) With your left hand, grab the back of your attacker's collar (or his hair). Your right palm rests behind his right knee joint, thumb down. (3) Press the nerve just inside his gastrocnemius muscle (see inset 3A) behind the knee joint. This will cause his leg to jerk up automatically. If this doesn't work, try pinching the inside of the attacker's thigh very quickly just above the knee joint with the nails of your right thumb and index finger. (4) As he lifts his leg, continue to raise it farther. At the same time, pivot your left leg back and out of the way as you yank down on his collar. (5) Follow your attacker down to the ground (in case he keeps hold with the head lock), dropping onto your left knee. (6-7) Grab his groin with your right hand and pull.

CROSS-LAPEL WHEEL THROW

Eri Nage/Juji Makikomi

(1) Your attacker grabs your clothing with both hands. (2) Bring your left hand up and grab the attacker's left lapel as high as possible, your palm facing out. Then grab his opposite lapel at about midchest height with your right hand. (3) Pull your attacker toward you with your right hand to set the choke. (It is not necessary to push with your left hand to set the choke. Let your right hand do

all the work.) (4) Step back with your left foot as you pivot to your left to throw. Your right hand should continue pulling his right lapel, and your left forearm should be firmly lodged under his chin, choking him. (5) Go down onto your left knee to finish the throw. (6) Pull up on his right lapel with your right hand to choke. Your left knee should be against the back of his head for support.

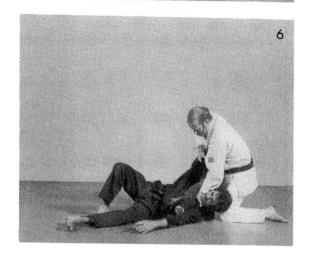

Technique:
SHOULDER-LOCK HIP THROW
Ude Guruma Ogoshi

Submission:
WRIST-LOCK-LIFT SUBMISSION
Tekubi Shimi Waza

(1) Your attacker attempts a knife swipe. (2) Lean back slightly, and sidestep to your left to get out of the path of his knife. (3) Once the knife has passed, move back in and make a fist with both hands, (4) step in with your right foot and bring both forearms up to block his back swing. (5) Block hard. (Fists are needed here because of his much greater force with a back swing.) Your left forearm should block above the attacker's elbow, while your right forearm blocks his lower forearm as close to his elbow as possible. (This will help keep your right forearm away from the knife blade.) (6) Before your opponent recovers from the blow, bend his arm by pushing with your right forearm. Do not grab his forearm with your right hand because he will be able to resist if you do. Open your right hand as you bend his arm back.

Continued on next page

(7) Bring your left forearm over his upper arm and clamp onto your right forearm. (The hold is shown more clearly in step 9). At this point you may execute a rear shoulder-lock takedown (not shown) by pushing down with your right forearm and stepping forward with your right leg, then going down onto your right knee, as on page 67. (8) To execute a hip throw, swing your body around, bringing your left foot back against your opponent with your right hip blocking his. Hold the shoulder lock tight against you. (9) Execute the throw, going down onto your right knee. (10) To set a wrist-lock lift, slide your right hand down to the back of his hand so his knuckles are resting in the palm of your hand. (11) Lift up at the knuckles to break his wrist (12) or to raise your opponent up so you can set a neck scissor along with the wrist lock. (13) Lean back to set the scissor.

This chart shows specific techniques in this book that can be applied to a variety of attacks. While there would be no modification in the actual execution of the specific technique, it would be necessary to modify your initial response (for example: block, release, strike, etc.) to the specific attack from what was shown in the text.

BASIC JUJITSU TECHNIQUES

Technique	single lapel	double lapel	front choke	rear choke	rear forearm choke	head lock	rear shoulder grab	rear bear hug
Basic One-Arm Hip Throw	✓	✓	✓	✓	✓	✓	✓	✓
Basic Drop Throw	✓	✓	✓	✓	✓	✓	✓	✓
Leg Lift					✓		✓	
Drop Throw	✓	✓	✓	✓	✓		✓	
Throat (Trachea) Attack	✓	✓	✓					
Chin or Nose Turn						✓		
Basic Hand Throw	✓	✓	✓			✓		
Outer Sweeping Hip Throw	✓	✓	✓	✓	✓	✓	✓	✓
Corkscrew						✓		
Armbar Rear Throw								
Armbar Winding Throw	✓	✓						
Outer Rear-Sweeping Hip Throw	✓							
Neck Throw	✓	✓	✓				✓	
Inner-Sweeping Hip Throw	✓	✓	✓		✓		✓	✓
Stomach Throw	✓	✓	✓					
Floating Drop Throw								
Forward Finger Throw						✓		✓
Body Winding Throw	✓	✓					✓	✓
Leg-Lift Throw								
Inner Rear-Sweeping Throw	✓	✓						
Knuckle-Press Takedown	✓							
Wrist-Lock-Lift Come-Along								
Nerve Wheel Throw	✓	✓	✓					
Thumb Winding Throw				✓				
Sleeve Pivot Throw								
Wrist-Lock Takedown	✓	✓					✓	✓
Shoulder-Lock Rear Takedown								
Shoulder-Lock Come-Along								
Elbow-Turn Takedown	✓	✓	✓					
Elbow-Roll Takedown								
Elbow Lift								
Head Winding Throw	✓	✓	✓	✓				
Lapel Wheel Throw	✓	✓	✓					
Hip Throw								

DIFFERENT TYPES OF ATTACKS

front bear hug	single hit	double hit	overhead club	sideswipe club	overhead knife	straight knife	knife swipe	handshake	wrist grab	kick	push	grab and hit	hair grab	mugging	arm grab
✓	✓	✓	✓	✓				✓	✓		✓	✓		✓	
✓	✓	✓	✓					✓	✓	✓	✓	✓		✓	
														✓	
✓														✓	
✓	✓	✓	✓					✓	✓	✓		✓			
✓	✓	✓	✓	✓	✓	✓			✓						
✓	✓	✓		✓					✓		✓	✓		✓	
✓	✓	✓		✓				✓	✓						
			✓		✓										
✓	✓	✓	✓									✓			
✓	✓	✓										✓			
✓	✓	✓	✓						✓			✓			
✓	✓	✓							✓			✓			
✓	✓								✓		✓	✓			
✓		✓													
✓	✓							✓	✓			✓			
✓	✓	✓	✓				✓								
										✓					
✓	✓	✓								✓					
													✓		
													✓		
													✓		
✓		✓							✓						
✓		✓		✓					✓			✓			
							✓								
							✓								
✓	✓														
														✓	
															✓
✓	✓											✓			
				✓			✓								
✓				✓			✓								

Photo by Thomas Sanders

CHAPTER 5
SCORING CRITERIA FOR
RANK (BELT) EXAMINATIONS

Changing Criteria

When I first started teaching jujitsu in the 1960s, it was during a time when a sensei could conduct his dojo in a traditional manner, which did not include a specified list of skills to be accomplished for each belt rank. Seki would make promotions based on more than just technical skills and proficiency—he also looked at the person. What common jujitsu skills did the student possess? What was his learning curve? What was his attitude? Would he make a good representative of the art? This type of subjective evaluation was entirely acceptable in the 1960s and 1970s, and I used the same approach. My students accepted the evaluation process because it seemed fair even though it was subjective. There was some common knowledge that I expected each student at a certain rank level to know, but otherwise nothing was specifically written down.

This method worked well until I approached the principal of Olive Vista Jr. High School in Sylmar, Calif. At the time, I was a history teacher in the school and the creator of its after-school jujitsu program. Within a year, the program had become so popular that I thought it would be a good idea to incorporate it into the regular school curriculum as an alternative to physical education classes or as an elective for students. The principal, Richard Miles, had a strong belief in innovation and liked my proposal. However, I had to do something first: establish "objective and measurable skills for student performance." This translated into specific belt-rank requirements, but it also meant I had to come up with a standard means of measurement for each technique.

The belt-rank requirements in the original *Jujitsu: Basic Techniques of the Gentle Art* were a result of formalizing objective belt-rank requirements so that I could teach a jujitsu class in a public school. At the time, there were five ranks below shodan, or first-degree black belt. They were sixth *kyu* (green belt), fourth kyu (purple belt) and third, second and first kyu (three levels of brown belt.) There was no official fifth kyu (green belt with a yellow stripe) test, but I sometimes gave them out to students who had tried really hard to pass the purple-belt exam but didn't make it. I also sometimes awarded the fifth kyu to a sixth-kyu student who was working really hard and needed encouragement. The fifth kyu was a subjective promotion in either case.

Also following in the tradition of Seki, I would sometimes award a seventh kyu (yellow belt) to a younger student who had tried to pass the sixth-kyu exam but wasn't successful. It was another subjective belt meant to instill a certain level of encouragement in the student.

Even though I had the best of intentions and thought I'd planned out the progression of belt-rank requirements smoothly, I hit two problems. The first was that I had a high failure rate among students who tested for fourth kyu. They rarely passed the test the first time; generally, they had to test two to four times to be successful. This was very frustrating for the students and caused them to dropout at a fast rate. The second was in providing some consistent guidance to students in terms of subjective criteria.

I solved this problem in the mid-1980s by tasking a brown belt and a black belt of mine to look over the problem. Their conclusions, like mine, showed that there were simply too many techniques students had to perform. The learning demand was too great to move up from a sixth kyu to a fourth kyu. In fact, it was a much bigger learning curve than that required for a third kyu. So I tasked my helpers with a second assignment: Come up with a formal fifth-kyu exam. Essentially, I was telling them to split the fourth-kyu exam in half and balance each out with rank-appropriate kata.

What you see in this expanded edition of the book are the fruits of my students' labor. They revised the fifth- and fourth-kyu learning criteria and exams and solved my high dropout rate with an unexpected bonus. Now, when students pass the fourth-kyu test, they have greater technical proficiency in more techniques. This was a win-win situation for everyone.

In regards to the second problem, establishing common ground for subject criteria, I began to let lower belt-rank students know I was evaluating their "attitudes." I did not have any "attitude" scores for the more advanced third through first, or *dan*, grades because I figured the students understood that they wouldn't be up for promotion unless they had the proper attitude. But what was the "attitude" I was looking for? Was I going to completely "objectify" my promotional criteria with another "long" list of specifics? Or was I going to keep the criteria as general as possible? There are two things that affected how I was going to look at a student's attitude at any belt level: simplicity and the "rule of three."

When I started out as a teacher, I thought having a lot of rules would be more effective in establishing class control. But I soon noticed that I wound up wasting a lot of instructional time enforcing those rules. I also saw that teachers who had very few behavioral rules spent more time teaching and interacting with their students, to everyone's benefit. So I took a leap. I came up with a single acronym rule: TR2. It stood for the following: "Think before you act. Be **r**esponsible for what you do. Be **t**olerant of others. **R**espect the rights of others as you would like them to respect you." Eventually, I was able to reduce it to one general statement on how I ran my regular classes and my jujitsu classes: Respect each other as equals, and treat others as you would like to be treated.

This one rule made classroom management, as well as dojo management, a lot easier. However, I still needed something that worked with budoshin jujitsu. The "rule of three" helped provide the solution. I first learned about the "rule of three" in my debate classes in high school, and it was reinforced in my speech and debate classes in college. The "rule of three" states that the human psyche is most accepting of an idea or position if you can provide three examples or three pieces of evidence to support your position. If you only offer one to two pieces of evidence, it seems insufficient. For some reason, three seems to be satisfying, as in, mind-body-spirit, or life-liberty-and-the-pursuit-of-happiness, or introduction-body-conclusion elements in writing. Perhaps it's because it's the smallest number that can be used to create a closed pattern—a triangle. Anyway, I looked into the meaning of budoshin and came up with three components: integrity, humility and respect. In jujitsu, none of these elements can function independently of the others. I will explain each one as simply as possible so you will know where I'm coming from when I look at a student's attitude.

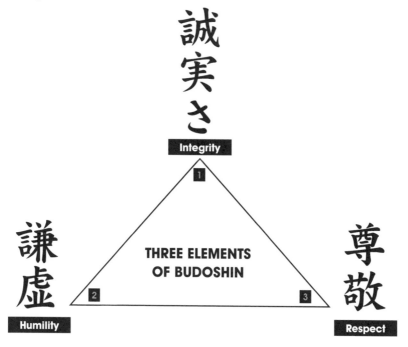

1. Integrity can be defined as your reputation, how you see yourself and, more important, how other people see you. This is usually a long-term view of you based on your history. Are you trustworthy? Are you reliable? Do you deal honestly with yourself and others? Do you have a code of conduct that other people will respect and follow you for? Will you lead by example? All these things combine to create your self-image and your sense of integrity. They are based on your sense of respect and humility.

2. Humility is your ability to be humble while maintaining your integrity. You do not need to be boastful or tell people how wonderful you are or how much you know or what you can do. Although you may be quite knowledgeable or competent, it is for others to discover through your behavior, your actions and their experiences with you. It is your ability to sincerely apologize when you have erred and help others who are in need without expecting thanks or compensation. Humility is based on your sense of integrity and respect for yourself and others.

3. Respect influences your perception of yourself and how others perceive you. It is how you treat others and how they treat you. It is about how you would like to be treated by other people. If others see that you respect yourself, then they will respect you. Respect is never something you can innately expect or demand from others. Nor should respect be confused with obedience. A person may obey you and yet not respect you. On the other hand, if they respect you, they are more likely to obey you because they know you are acting in their best interest. Respect is something that must be earned and maintained by maintaining your sense of integrity and humility.

All three of these values combine to form the subjective "attitude" score. They are at least as important as the technical and self-defense skills you will learn as a student of jujitsu, or any martial art, because with the effective knowledge of a martial art comes responsibility. By conducting yourself in a respectful manner with integrity and humility, you will serve as an example to others; you will not abuse your martial arts knowledge, and other people will see you as the credible and responsible person that you are.

By making these three values part of your life philosophy, you will also be a happier, more accepting and more successful person in your life because you will have developed an inner sense of confidence that doesn't have to be proved.

Last, from a martial arts viewpoint, jujitsu has the potential of being a very devastating martial art, so the serious student also must have a strong philosophy of life as an effective counterbalance to the potential damage he/she can inflict on an assailant. As an instructor of the art, I have the additional responsibility of trying to have my students develop a life philosophy that encompasses integrity, humility and respect in whatever they do in life. I have tried to follow this philosophy myself, and the payback has been tremendous.

When you see the belt-rank requirements that follow, you will notice some major changes that did not appear in the original publication of this book:

A *gokyu* belt sequence has been added to the instructional sequence. This also resulted in substantial belt-requirement changes to the *yonkyu* exam and minor changes to the *sankyu, nikyu*, and *ikkyu* exams.

The "attitude" on all belt exams, although still a subjective measure, is more clearly defined than before. Rather than a vague interpretation, students now have a better idea of what I'm looking for.

A reference column containing cross-references to my book series by Black Belt and my Panther series of eight DVDs has been added to each of the Technique Sequence pages. Now students are able to accurately see the techniques I am requiring at each belt level. The cross-reference coding used in the Technique Sequence pages is relatively easy to follow. In each sequence, there is a reference column. For example, on page 136, you will find the *ube shioku waza* in the "kata" column on the green-belt sequence. The technique in English is the "thumb-tip press." The reference column refers to the code "V1-12" and "N-180." "V1" refers to the first DVD of the Panther DVD video series *Budoshin Jujitsu Black Belt Home Study Course*. And "12" means that this is the 12th technique shown on the first DVD. "N-180" means that the technique also can be found on page 180 of the book *Jujitsu Nerve Techniques*, also written by me.

Additional coding works as follows: V1 = first DVD, V2 = second DVD, etc. The letter "B" refers to this volume of *Jujitsu: Basic Techniques of the Gentle Art*, and the letter "I" refers to the book *Jujitsu: Intermediate Techniques of the Gentle Art*. The page number, on which the technique description is presented, follows the letter B, I or N. This presents a nice cross-referencing package you can use to make sure you are learning the correct techniques for each belt sequence.

Last, rather than just presenting the belt exams, as was done in the original version of this book, I am also including the technique sequence for each belt. You will notice that more techniques are listed in the technique sequence than what is required in the kata portion of the test. The balance of these techniques, or techniques learned for prior belt-rank promotional exams, may be used for the waza portion of the test.

General-Knowledge Requirements for 6/Rokyu to 1/Ikkyu Technique Sequences and Belt Exams

ROKYU (Green Belt) 15-30 instruction hours and training time	
Y / N	Can tie obi correctly.
Y / N	Can show proper method of rolling up gi and tying it formally.
Y / N	Knows the 10 basic situations in which a student is to bow.
Y / N	Can define "jujitsu" very briefly.
Y / N	Can count from 1 to 10 in Japanese.

GOKYU (Blue Belt) 25-50 instruction hours and training time	
Y / N	Can meet all previous general-knowledge requirements.
Y / N	Can explain proper etiquette and behavior in dealing with higher ranks and black belts.

YONKYU (Purple Belt) 20-50 instruction hours and training time	
Y / N	Can meet all previous general-knowledge requirements.
Y / N	Can explain proper etiquette and behavior in dealing with higher ranks and black belts.

Questions for the rank of sankyu and higher will be graded on a score of 1 to 5 (5 being the best). Those being tested for sankyu must achieve a score of 15 or better; nikyu 30 or better; ikkyu 55 or better. All "Y"s also must be circled.

SANKYU (Brown Belt with Green Stripe) 50-100 instruction hours and training time	
Y / N	Can meet all previous general-knowledge requirements (MUST be explored).
Y / N	Sets a positive example for lower ranks.
Y / N	Assists in the instructional program.
/ 10	Can explain the relative advantages of judo, karate and aikido in jujitsu.
/ 10	Can show 10 different nerves on the human body.
/ 20	TOTAL

NIKYU (Brown Belt with Black Stripe) 50-100 instruction hours and training time	
Y / N	Can meet all previous general-knowledge requirements (MUST be explored).
Y / N	Sets a positive example for lower ranks.
Y / N	Assists in the instructional program.
/ 5	Can explain the relative advantages of judo, karate and aikido in jujitsu.
/ 5	Can show 10 different nerves on the human body.
/ 30	Sensei to choose 6 of the following at random:
/ 5	Define jujitsu.
/ 5	Explain the use of ki in jujitsu.
/ 5	Explain the philosophy of jujitsu.
/ 5	Explain the five steps of learning. (See pages 28 to 29 in *Jujitsu: Intermediate Techniques of the Gentle Art* .)

/ 5	Explain the circle theory.
/ 5	Explain the tori's relationship to the uke.
/ 5	What is your responsibility to lower-ranked classmates?
/ 5	What four actions make up a complete jujitsu waza?
/ 5	How does one develop agility and flexibility?
/ 5	Random question.
/ 40	**TOTAL**

IKKYU (Brown Belt with Blue Stripe) 50-100 instruction hours and training time	
Y / N	Can meet all previous general-knowledge requirements (MUST be explored).
Y / N	Sets a positive example for lower ranks.
Y / N	Assists in the instructional program.
Y / N	Has potential as an instructor.
Y / N	Is certified as a mat referee.
/ 5	Can explain the relative advantages of judo, karate and aikido in jujitsu.
/ 5	Can show 10 different nerves on the human body.
/ 30	Sensei to choose 6 of the following at random:
/ 5	Define jujitsu.
/ 5	What is your responsibility to lower-ranked classmates?
/ 5	Explain the philosophy of jujitsu.
/ 5	How does one develop agility and flexibility?
/ 5	Explain the circle theory.
/ 5	Explain the tori's relationship to the uke.
/ 5	Explain the use of ki in jujitsu.
/ 5	What four actions make up a complete jujitsu waza?
/ 5	Explain the five steps of learning.
/ 5	Random question.
/30	Sensei to choose 6 of the following at random for definition and explanation:
/ 5	Aiki
/ 5	Mudansha
/ 5	Yudansha
/ 5	Budoshin
/ 5	Mushin
/ 5	Random question
/ 5	Kiai
/ 5	Saiki Tanden
/ 5	Kuzushi
/ 5	Sutemi
/ 70	**TOTAL**

Physical Performance Scoring Criteria for All Mat Exams

SCORE	EXPLANATION	EXAMPLES
0	Unable to execute	Unable to execute technique or wrong technique executed.
1	Poor	Must be told or shown how technique is done. Barely able to execute technique. Severe loss of balance.
2	Very awkward	Very awkward execution of technique. Poor balance. Verbal assistance required. Technique or moves must be repeated at least once.
3	Barely effective, awkward	Somewhat awkward. Poor balance. Some verbal assistance required. Probably repeats or has to repeat moves or techniques.
4	Effective but awkward	Technique done fairly smoothly. Little hesitation in movements. Good balance. No verbal assistance required. No repetitions of moves or techniques.
5	Good, very smooth	Technique done very smoothly. Well-balanced. No hesitation displayed at any time. Returns to tachi waza. Kiai and/or appropriate submission.
6	Very good, fluid	Exceptionally good form. Very fluid movement. Kiai and return to tachi waza. Submission suitable for technique.
7	Excellent, an art	Excellent form and execution. Jujitsu as an art.

6/ROKYU (GREEN BELT) TECHNIQUE SEQUENCE		
KATA	TECHNIQUE	REFERENCE
Yoko Ukemi	Side Fall	V1 B-36
Ushiro Ukemi	Back Fall	V1 B-38
Mae Ukemi	Forward Roll Fall	V1 B-40, 42
Koshi Nage	Basic Hip Throw	V1-1 B-46
Tekubi Shimi Waza	Wrist-Lock Takedown	V2-6 B-98
Te No Tatake	Blocking (Blocking Portion of Tai-Otoshi)	V1 B-48
Juji	Cross-Blocking (Blocking Portion of Ude Guruma)	V1 B-64
Te Tatake	Striking Technique	V1 B-46
Te Nage	Hand Throw	V1-5 B-58
Shioku Waza	Nerve Technique (Larynx Press)	V1-6 B-54
Ashi Tatake	Foot Strike and Lift	V1-8 B-50
Tai-Otoshi	Basic Drop Throw	V1-3 B-48
Atama Makikomi	Head Winding Throw (Key Turn)	V1-9 B-116
Shimi Waza with Hiji Tatake	Chin or Nose Turn	V1-10 B-56
Ude Guruma Ushiro	Shoulder-Lock Rear Takedown	V1-11 B-100
Ube Shioku Waza	Thumb-Tip Press	V1-12 N-180

6/ROKYU (GREEN BELT) MAT EXAM		
TECHNIQUE	**SCORE**	**COMMENT**
Mae Ukemi (Forward Roll Fall)		
Yoko Ukemi (Side Fall)		
Ushiro Ukemi (Back Fall)		
TOTAL UKEMI	**/ 21**	**MINIMUM 12 / 21 TO CONTINUE**
Koshi Nage (Basic Hip Throw)		
Tai-Otoshi (Basic Drop Throw)		
Te No Tatake (Blocking Hits)		
Juji (Cross-Blocking)		
Shioku Waza (Nerve Technique)		
Te Tatake (Striking Technique)		
Te Nage (Basic Hand Throw)		
TOTAL KATA	**/ 49**	**TOTAL KATA**
Hit		
Hit		
Shirt Grab		
Body Grab or Head Lock		
Front Choke		
TOTAL WAZA	**/ 35**	**TOTAL WAZA**
ATTITUDE	**/ 28**	**ATTITUDE**
KATA, WAZA AND ATTITUDE GRAND TOTAL	**/ 133**	**MINIMUM PASSING SCORE 93 (70%)**

5/GOKYU (BLUE BELT) TECHNIQUE SEQUENCE

KATA	TECHNIQUE	REFERENCE	
Kubi Nage with Kubi Shimi Waza	Neck Throw with Scissor-Choke Submission	V2-1	B-72
Kubi Shioku Waza	Side Neck Standing Submission	V2-2	I-134
Ashi Waza	Ankle Block	V2-3	NA
Osoto Gari	Outer-Sweeping Rear Throw	V2-4	B-70
Shioku Ashi Ushiro Nage	Nerve-Attack Rear Circle Throw (Rear Leg Lift)	V2-5	B-118
Tekubi Shimi Waza	Wrist-Lock Takedown	V2-6	B-98
Ude Guruma	Corkscrew	V2-7	B-64
Mae Yubi Nage	Forward Finger Throw	V2-15	B-80
Ude Guruma	Shoulder-Lock Come-Along	V2-8	B-102
Kime-No-Kata	Focus Techniques	NA	
Sode Otoshi	Sleeve-Hold Knee-Drop Throw	V2-9	I-144
Tai-Otoshi with Te Tatake	Drop Throw with Cheek Strike	V2-10	B-52
Shioku Waza	Nerve Attack Wheel	V2-11	B-92
Hiji Waza	Elbow-Roll Takedown	V2-12	B-104
Ude Guruma Makikomi	Armbar Winding Throw	V2-14	B-68
Ude Guruma Makikomi with Hasami	Armbar Winding Throw with Scissor Submission	V2-13	B-106
Kime-No-Kata	Focus Techniques	NA	
Ippon Seoi Nage	One-Arm Hip Throw	V1-1	B-46
Ube Shioku Waza	Thumb-Tip Press	V1-12	N-180
Te Shimi Waza	Knuckle-Press Takedown	V2-15	B-88
Kime-No-Kata	Focus Techniques	NA	

5/GOKYU MAT EXAM

DEMONSTRATION INCLUDES 2—4 SUBMISSIONS OR COME-ALONGS

TECHNIQUE	SCORE	COMMENT
Ippon Seoi Nage (One-Arm Hip Throw)		
Yubi Nage (Finger Throw)		
Osoto Gari (Outside-Sweeping Rear Throw)		
Ude Guruma Makikomi (Armbar Winding Throw]		
Tai-Otoshi (Drop Throw)		
Ude Guruma (Corkscrew)		
Hiji Waza (Elbow Technique)		
Shioku Waza (Nerve Technique)		
Kubi Nage (Neck Throw)		
Kime-No-Kata No. 1 (Free Choice)		
Kime-No-Kata No. 2 (Free Choice)		
TOTAL KATA	**/ 77**	**TOTAL KATA**
Handshake		
Front Choke		
Bear Hug		
Rear Waist Grab		
Hair Grab		
Lapel Grab		
Wrist Grab		
Right or Left Hit		
Rear Shoulder Grab		
Clothing Grab		
Head Lock		
Freestyle Attack No. 1		
Freestyle Attack No. 2		
TOTAL WAZA	**/ 91**	**TOTAL WAZA**
ATTITUDE	**/ 28**	**ATTITUDE**
KATA, WAZA AND ATTITUDE GRAND TOTAL	**/ 196**	**MINIMUM PASSING SCORE 137 (70%)**

4/YONKYU (PURPLE BELT) TECHNIQUE SEQUENCE

KATA	TECHNIQUE	REFERENCE	
Harai Goshi	Outer-Sweeping Hip Throw	V3-1	B-60
Ude Guruma Ushiro with Ude Gatame	Armbar (Shoulder-Lock) Rear Throw	V3-2	B-66
Tomoe Nage with Eri Shimi Waza	Stomach Throw with Lapel-Choke Submission	V3-3	B-76
Ude Guruma Makikomi	Armbar Winding Throw	V2-14	B-68
Kime-No-Kata	Focus Techniques	NA	
Te Nage	Hand Throw	I-118	
Tekubi Yoko Nage	Wrist Side Throw	V3-5	I-102
Ushiro Nage	Leg-Lift Rear Throw	V3-6	B-84
Uchi Gari	Inner Rear-Sweeping Throw	V4-4	B-86
Hiki Yoko Nage	Sleeve Pivot Throw	V3-7	B-96
Ude Guruma	Shoulder-Lock Come-Along	B-102	
Uki Otoshi with Ude Guruma	Floating Drop Throw with Shoulder-Lock Pin	V3-8	B-78
Kime-No-Kata	Focus Techniques	NA	
Makikomi with Ude Guruma	Body Winding Throw to Shoulder-Lock Pin	V3-9	B-82
Ube Makikomi	Thumb Winding Throw	V3-11	B-94
Kime-No-Kata	Focus Techniques	NA	
Hane Goshi with Hiza Tatake	Inner-Sweeping Hip Throw with Knee-Drop Submission	V3-12	B-74
Eri Nage (Juji Makikomi)	Lapel Wheel Throw	V3-14	B-120

4/YONKYU MAT EXAM

DEMONSTRATION INCLUDES 2—4 SUBMISSIONS OR COME-ALONGS

TECHNIQUE	SCORE	COMMENT
Harai Goshi or Hane Goshi (Outer-Sweeping Hip Throw or Inner-Sweeping Hip Throw)		
Tomoe Nage (Stomach Throw)		
Uki Otoshi (Floating Drop Throw)		
Ude Guruma Ushiro (Shoulder-Lock Rear Takedown)		
Ude Guruma Makikomi (Armbar Winding Throw)		
Shioku Waza (Nerve Technique)		
Tekubi Shimi Waza (Wrist-Lock Come-Along)		
Te Nage (Hand Throw)		
Hiki Yoko Nage (Sleeve Pivot Throw)		
Eri Nage (Lapel Wheel Throw)		
Ushiro Nage (Leg-Lift Rear Throw)		
Kime-No-Kata No. 1 (Free Choice)		
Kime-No-Kata No. 2 (Free Choice)		
TOTAL KATA	**/ 91**	**TOTAL KATA**
Double Hit		
Lapel Grab and Hit		
Handshake		
One-Arm Rear Forearm Choke		
Kick No. 1		
Kick No. 2		
Knife Attack No. 1		
Knife Attack No. 2		
Rear Neck Grab or Rear Choke		
Club Attack		
Double Wrist Grab		
Hit to Stomach		
Freestyle Attack No. 1		
Freestyle Attack No. 2		
TOTAL WAZA	**/ 98**	**TOTAL WAZA**
ATTITUDE	**/ 28**	**ATTITUDE**
KATA, WAZA AND ATTITUDE GRAND TOTAL	**/ 217**	**MINIMUM PASSING SCORE 152 (70%)**

3/SANKYU (BROWN BELT/GREEN STRIPE) TECHNIQUE SEQUENCE

KATA	TECHNIQUE	REFERENCE	
Hiki Waza (Mae Ushiro Nage)	Pulling Technique (Forward Rear Throw)	V4-1	I-124
Te Waza	Hand Throw/Technique	V4-2	I-118
Ude Makikomi	Winding Armbar Takedown	V4-3	I-132
Ouchi Gari	Inner Sweeping Rear Throw	V4-4	B-86
Tekubi Shimi Waza	Wrist-Lock Come-Along	V4-5	I-168
Ushiro Nage	Leg-Lift Rear Throw	V3-6	B-84
Hiji Waza	Hand Wind Forward Elbow-Roll Takedown	V4-6	B-112
Hiji Waza	Elbow-Roll Takedown	V8-20	B-110
Ashi Yoko Nage (with Ashi Guruma)	Foot-Twist Winding Throw	V4-7	I-96
Obi Nage	Belt Throw	V4-8	I-88
Mae Yubi Nage (with Yubi Shimi Waza)	Forward Finger Throw with Finger-Press Submission	V4-9	I-150
Atama Otoshi	Hair Grab Drop Throw	V4-10	I-152
Ura Nage	Rear Circle Throw	V4-11	I-116
Hiji Waza	Elbow-Lift Come-Along (or Rear Throw)	V4-12	B-114
Eri Nage	Lapel Wheel Throw	V3-14	B-120
Shioku Waza	Rear Leg-Lift Throw	B-118	
Uki Otoshi	Reverse Throws (Floating Drop Throw)	V4-13	I-176
Tekubi Shimi Waza (with Ude Guruma)	Wrist-Lock-Lift Come-Along and Arm-Lock Come-Along	B-90	
Senaka Hiki Nage	Reverse Throws (Shoulder Pull Throw)	V4-14	I-178
Ashi Tatake	Reverse Throws (Leg-Strike Rear Takedown)	V4-15	I-180
Ura Nage	Shoulder Grab Rear Throw	V4-20	I-80
Ude Guruma	Shoulder-Lock Hip Throw	V4-16	B-122
Ura Harai	Outer-Sweeping Rear Throw	V4-21	I-136
Ura Nage	Rear Throw	V4-17	I-122
Kao Tatake	Face Attack	V4-18	I-156
Hidari Te Nage	Left Hand Throw	V4-19	I-154
Kime-No-Kata	Focus Techniques (review previously learned techniques)	NA	

2/NIKYU (BROWN BELT WITH BLACK STRIPE) TECHNIQUE SEQUENCE

ADDITIONAL TECHNIQUES FOR NIKYU

KATA	TECHNIQUE	REFERENCE	
Te Waza	Hand Throw/Technique (Sutemi Waza)	V6-10	
Ude Makikomi	Winding Armbar Takedown (Sutemi Waza)	V6-11	
Tekubi Shimi Waza	Wrist-Lock Come-Along (Sutemi Waza)	V6-9	
Hiji Waza	Hand Wind Forward Elbow-Roll Takedown	V5-1	
Ashi Yoko Nage (with Ashi Guruma)	Foot-Twist Winding Throw (for foot stomp on ground)	V6-4	I-202
Ura Nage	Knee-Lock Rear Throw (leg grab and pull)	V5-4	I-204
Ago No Maki Shimi Waza	Chin Wind Reverse Pin (for head lock on ground)	V6-6	I-216
Ashi Tatake	Reverse Throws (Leg-Strike Rear Takedown)	V5-8	I-200
Ude Guruma	Shoulder-Lock Pin (Ground reverse for attempted figure-4 lock)	V6-7	I-218

1/IKKYU (BROWN BELT WITH BLUE STRIPE) TECHNIQUE SEQUENCE

ADDITIONAL TECHNIQUES FOR IKKYU

KATA	TECHNIQUE	REFERENCE
Te Waza	Hand Throw/Technique (Sutemi Waza optional)	V6-10
Tekubi Shimi Waza	Wrist-Lock Technique (Sutemi Waza optional)	V6-9
Mae Yubi Nage (with Yubi Shimi Waza)	Forward Finger Throw Finger-Press Submission (Sutemi)	V6-12
Ude Guruma	Armbar Winding Throw (Sutemi Waza optional)	V6-11

3 to 1/SANKYU to IKKYU MAT EXAM: KATA PORTION

IKKYU CANDIDATES: FREESTYLE KATA REQUIREMENT

You will be expected to demonstrate responses to continuous random attacks (at moderate speed) by an uke for 30 to 60 seconds, demonstrating your ability to use jujitsu techniques as a means of effective self-defense.

DEMONSTRATION INCLUDES 2 to 4 SUBMISSIONS OR COME-ALONGS

(You may not use a specific submission more than two times in the kata portion or more than two times in the waza portion of the mat test for ikkyu.)

KATA (EXAMINER TO CHOOSE 15 FROM CHOICES BELOW)		
TECHNIQUE	**SCORE**	**COMMENT**
Koshi Nage (Hip Throw)		
Tai-Otoshi (Drop Throw)		
Ura Nage (Rear Throw)		
Ouchi Gari (Inner Rear-Sweeping Throw)		
Shioku Waza (Nerve Technique)		
Te Tatake (Striking Technique)		
Te Nage (Hand Throw)		
Ippon Seoi Nage (One-Arm Hip Throw)		
Harai Goshi (Outer-Sweeping Hip Throw)		
Hane Goshi (Inner-Sweeping Hip Throw)		
Tomoe Nage (Stomach Throw)		
Uki Otoshi (Floating Drop Throw)		
Yubi Nage (Finger Throw)		
Makikomi (Winding Throw)		
Ude Guruma (Shoulder-Lock Come-Along)		
Ude Guruma Ushiro (Shoulder-Lock Rear Takedown)		
Osoto Gari (Outer-Sweeping Rear Throw)		
Kubi Nage (Neck Throw)		
Te Waza (Hand Throw)		
Ashi Waza (Ankle Block)		
Hiji Waza (Elbow-Roll Takedown)		
Shimi Waza (Pain/Strangling Technique)		
Hiki Waza (Pulling Technique)		
Kubi Shimi Waza (Neck-Strangling Technique)		
TOTAL KATA	**/ 70**	**TOTAL KATA**

3 to 1 /SANKYU to IKKYU MAT EXAM: WAZA (SELF-DEFENSE) PORTION

DEMONSTRATION INCLUDES 2—4 SUBMISSIONS OR COME-ALONGS

(You may not use a specific submission more than two times in the kata portion or more than two times in the waza portion of the mat test for ikkyu.)

WAZA (EXAMINER TO CHOOSE 15 FROM CHOICES BELOW)		
TECHNIQUE	SCORE	COMMENT
Club Attacks		
Kicks		
Handholds		
Arm Lock		
Head Lock		
Reversing a Throw		
Being Pulled		
Football Tackle		
Double Hits		
Hair Grabs		
Knife Attacks		
Lapel Grab		
Combination Holds and Attacks		
Cross-Choke		
Multiple Attackers		
Bear Hugs and Waist Grabs		
Rear Nelson		
Knife Threat		
Chokes		
Handshakes		
Baton Attacks		
Reversing Opponent on Mat		
Shoulder Grabs		
Miscellaneous Clothing Grabs		
Ground Defenses		
TOTAL WAZA	**/ 105**	**TOTAL WAZA**
KATA AND WAZA GRAND TOTAL	**/ 175**	**MINIMUM PASSING SCORE 131 (75%)**

Closing Points on Rokyu to Ikkyu Technique Sequences and Belt Exams

Once you have gone through the prior belt requirements you may be asking yourself two questions: Why did I present all the kyu-grade belt exams if this book only covers the sixth and fifth plus a few techniques for the fourth belt-rank exams? Also, why has a "general knowledge" requirement been added to all the kyu exams? These are legitimate questions, and they deserve complete answers.

In regards to the first question, it is my belief as a professional educator that students have a better chance of succeeding if presented with the entire course outline. It may seem like too much information, but most will appreciate it because when they know what their goals are, they know the whole picture. In other words, information is knowledge, and once you have knowledge of what will be required of you, you can make more effective decisions regarding your progress. There are no secrets, no hidden hurdles and no surprises. The learning process should be a smooth upward learning curve.

In regards to the second question, I never used to have a "general knowledge" requirement because my students assumed I would ask them to explain certain terms, whether one-on-one or in a more formal situation. And I assumed, or, more correctly, assumed *in*correctly that my black belts would continue my practice when they opened up their own dojo and trained their own students. Then, about 15 years ago, I was sitting on a black-belt promotional board and evaluating two candidates who were testing for black-belt grades—one for shodan and one for *nidan*. They both did exceptionally well on the mat-performance portion of the exam. I then asked the shodan candidate to explain ki and/or provide an example of how ki was properly used in the execution of any technique of their choice. The shodan candidate was unable to answer. I then asked the nidan candidate to explain what mushin was and how it applied to a self-defense situation. Again, the candidate was unable to respond to either part of the question.

As a result, I recommended that neither candidate be promoted because I believed these were really basic concepts that any person going for a black belt should know. In the end, the students were promoted by their sensei, but I decided that this type of embarrassing situation should not arise again. So, with a couple of my black belts, we sat down and came up with general-knowledge requirements that we believed would be realistic expectations for various belt levels.

As a unique twist to this new prerequisite, one of my black belts also suggested that this prerequisite testing be done by students one grade higher than the kyu grade the student is testing for. For example, a rokyu or gokyu student would test a white belt on their sixth belt-rank general-knowledge requirement. A nikyu or ikkyu would test a sankyu on the second belt-rank general-knowledge requirements. The tester also had to certify by signature that the testee knew the information.

This shared responsibility has worked beautifully. It continues the traditional theme in martial arts that higher ranks are responsible for lower ranks. It involves higher-ranked students in the evaluation of lower ranks. This helps students of different ranks develop a sense of respect and responsibility for each other. It also relieves the sensei of the additional burden. It was a win-win situation for everyone. Coincidentally, I had used this same process of pre-evaluation, or "peer review," in a public-school classroom for years but had never thought of applying it in my dojo. It took a student to come up with the idea. It also reinforced my belief that if you involve students in the instructional process, they can tremendously improve your abilities as a teacher.

Photo by Thomas Sanders

CHAPTER 6
HISTORY OF BUDOSHIN JUJITSU

Developing a More Complete History of Budoshin Jujitsu

When studying history, it's always important to remember that it is written by the victors of war rather than the vanquished. For example, the "westward movement" of the United States in the 18th and 19th centuries is common knowledge. However, not as many people know about "Manifest Destiny," which is the ideology that Americans used to justify their expansion into American Indian territory and their expulsion of the indigenous groups. The truth about the plight of the American Indian didn't really come to light until the publication of *Bury My Heart at Wounded Knee*[6] (1970), as well as subsequent books on the topic. All this is to say that true, fair and objective history is hard to find. Historians and writers do the best they can with the accessible information.

The story of Jack Sanzo Seki Haywood falls into the gray area of history. Like many great sensei who immigrated to the United States, Seki's history can't fully be verified. A lot of the information comes from oral history, as related by his senior black belts and students. A lot of the oral history is unverifiable because any written records, which might have verified Seki's life in Japan, were destroyed in World War II. However, even primary sources contacted in Japan indicated that there was a good probability that the oral history was relatively accurate. In the end, the oral history is probable, possible or, at the very worst, cannot be disproved. In the end, the decision of what is "true" belongs to you, the reader.

So why am I presenting a difficult-to-verify biography? My first reason is that I have a great deal of respect for Seki because he took me under his wing for so many years. He was persistent and patient. In presenting his biography, I have no intent in casting any disrespect to him. History is history, and he gave a lot to me. The second reason for researching and presenting his biography as accurately as possible is because it is the cornerstone for the history of budoshin jujitsu. Without Seki, budoshin jujitsu would not exist. There would be no instructional books and videos of this traditional martial art. At least that part of his "history," and the history of jujitsu, will be preserved for the future. I am proud to be part of that history and to preserve it for you and future generations of martial artists.

---

[6] *Bury My Heart at Wounded Knee* is by Dee Brown.

From left to right: William Fromm, Jack Sanzo Seki and George Kirby in the late 1960s.

Biography of Jack Sanzo Seki

Jack Sanzo Seki, whose legal name was changed to Jack M. Haywood in 1943, was born in Los Angeles on July 7, 1914. His father was a Japanese laborer in Los Angeles, according to a 2010 U.S. Census document. His mother was of Irish-American descent. Seki's father, Sanzo Seki (b. 1888—d. unverifiable) was a jujitsu master and took his son back to Japan at a very early age. However, he sent Seki to study under the legendary Jigoro Kano—an expert in *tenjin-shinyo-ryu jujitsu* and *kito-ryu* jujitsu and the founder of modern judo—instead of teaching his son himself. Some sources indicate that Seki was awarded a *sandan* in judo by Kano although there is no documentation available. After studying under Kano, Seki returned to master the art of jujitsu under his father's tutelage. Some sources indicate that Seki also earned an ikkyu grade in kendo, but that is also unverifiable. According to some sources, Seki may have attended Doshisha College in Kyoto, Japan.

Before World War II, Seki was given the option of being drafted into the Japanese army or returning to the United States, where he was a citizen by birth. Fortunately, he chose the latter and returned to the United States in the mid-1930s. With his martial arts training, some sources say that he worked for the U.S. Army Air Force as a weaponless defense instructor. Other sources claim that he served as a translator between captured Japanese soldiers and their American interrogators in the Pacific theater. Information as of October 2006, as released in official records under the Freedom of Information Act, shows that Seki served in the U.S. Army from 1941 to 1944. He was assigned to Company A, 34th Signal Training Battalion. He was awarded the American Defense Service Medal, World War II Victory Medal, World War II Service Lapel Button and a Good Conduct Medal. His rank was private, first class. Any additional records verifying that he was a weaponless defense instructor or was a translator or anything else he did in the military during World War II were destroyed in the 1973 fire at the Military Personnel Records Division of the National Personnel Records Center in St. Louis, Mo. The only other reliable source—the U.S. Army Signal Center in Fort Gordon, Ga.—indicates that the Company A, 34th Signal Training Battalion was stationed in Africa, Italy and Sicily. This casts some doubt on the verbal history that says Seki served as a translator in the Pacific theater, even though some Japanese-Americans were indeed used as translators during World War II.

After World War II, Seki went to work for what was then aircraft manufacturer Lockheed Corp. in Burbank, Calif. He worked as a manufacturing research mechanic from 1952 until his retirement in 1986. There is no specific information available about what Seki did during his 34 years at Lockheed. Seki then retired to Bullhead City, Ariz., where he worked for a helicopter company for a few years. In declining health from emphysema and severe pulmonary disease caused by years of smoking, Seki was eventually placed in a nursing home until he passed away on April 20, 1998.

Seki was an avid martial artist and dedicated instructor. His life revolved around jujitsu. He held *yudansha* grades in judo, karate, aikido, and jujitsu, most of which he earned in Japan. He was ultimately promoted to *kudan* or ninth dan in jujitsu. He taught at the Burbank YMCA in the early 1960s, then, in the mid-1960s, he moved his instructional program to Los Angeles Valley College where he taught jujitsu four nights a week for $1.25 per month. In the early 1980s, he moved his program to the Victory-Vineland Recreation Center in Van Nuys, Calif. When he retired from Lockheed in 1986, he also stopped actively teaching the art.

Seki was very demanding on the mat. Although his physical workouts were strenuous, his psychological demands on a student's mental attitude were even greater. He would ask a question. Usually a lower rank would answer the question first. Regardless of how inaccurate the answer, Seki would find some element in it that was deemed correct. If a middle rank then answered, the response might be considered more or less correct.

However, the higher you were in rank, the greater were your chances of being "wrong." The higher you were in rank, the more you were subjected to his verbal harassment, most often in front of the rest of the class. Brown and black belts were his No. 1 targets. I remember one night at class when we black belts decided not to answer any of Seki's questions to avoid criticism. But we met with no such luck. Seki spent the next five to 10 minutes chewing us out for not answering. All we could do was sit there and take it—or bow off the mat and never return. Seki did this to weed out students and black belts who would get upset with his harassment. Seki said many times that if your "ticky-ticky" gets hurt by what people say about you, you have no business being in the martial arts. He was up front with his students about this. None of his harassment was personal, although some students thought it was. This was his way of weeding out those who were weak in spirit and mind. He took this approach because jujitsu, as taught by Seki, was such a devastating martial art. He did not believe that students who couldn't control their emotions should study this gentle art.

Founding Budoshin Jujitsu

I initially began my formal study of jujitsu at the Burbank YMCA in the mid-1960s under one of Jack Seki's black belts. I didn't train directly under Seki until I began taking his classes at Valley College in 1967.

Like many traditional martial arts instructors, Seki never asked a student to do anything. He always commanded. So, in his usual manner, Seki approached William Fromm and me, who were both first-degree brown belts, to tell us that we would take over his Burbank YMCA program because the program, which was currently being taught by one of his black belts, was still under his control. We both protested because we were only brown belts, but Seki's response was, "Now you are black belts. Act like it." His only other comment was, "Bill knows more techniques [than you, George], and you're a professional teacher. You'll do fine."

Bam! We had become sensei.

The history of budoshin jujitsu is rather unique and recent compared to the history of most martial arts. Fromm and I took over the Burbank YMCA program without any further comments. In 1967, it was a relatively small program. Within a couple of years, we had an extremely large and solid program, which took up an entire gymnasium. By this time, other martial artists wanted to know what "style" of jujitsu we taught. Seki's attitude was that there was only jujitsu and that ultimately there weren't any styles—just variations on the theme.

With that thought in mind, Fromm and I came up with the name budoshin, which is a combination of *bu* (martial), *do* (way) and *shin* (spirit) and means "to conduct oneself in an honorable and respectable manner." The concept of budoshin is covered in much greater detail in my book *Jujitsu: Intermediate Techniques of the Gentle Art*. We also decided to call it budoshin jujitsu because it would be acceptable to our sensei, whereas he would object to budoshin-ryu jujitsu.

In the early 1970s, I had the opportunity to study under Harold Brosious who taught *ketsugo* jujitsu. Because I saw Seki and Brosious as traditional sensei, I made sure that both sensei knew I was training under them both and that I had their approval to proceed. Their only directive, inferred but unspoken, was that whatever I learned in one dojo stopped at the door of the other. I believed it was a reasonable and logical requirement. This also inferred no proselytizing of either art to the students of the other sensei.

Although Brosious had a radically different approach to teaching the art, many of his techniques supplemented and enriched what I had learned from Seki. Ketsugo did not use any Japanese terminology nor did it have the finesse that appeared in some of Seki's techniques. But it did work. It was extremely efficient, and it was very effective, even though some of the techniques were rather vicious. However, just like Seki, Brosious' teachings were based on street survival. Both believed that there were no rules for fighting. If you were physically attacked on the street, it was by someone who wasn't following the rules of society anyway. If your life is in danger, you have to do whatever it takes to protect your life. It's that simple. Thus, Seki and Brosious' teachings have been effectively incorporated into budoshin jujitsu.

There are different paths up the mountain. Many times, they cross and run parallel to each other. But the ultimate goal is the same. Both Sensei Seki and Brosious taught every technique from a street situation. Jujitsu was taught for self-defense. As students like myself progressed and our technique improved, both sensei helped the students make jujiitsu an art—to understand the theory and mechanics behind every move, how the human body acts and reacts, and how to incorporate that understanding into an extremely effective personalized self-defense system.

Historical Lineage

Sometimes it is easier to trace the lineage of a person, a series of historical events or even a martial art using a chart rather than presenting it solely in written form. In constructing the historical lineage chart that follows, I had two choices. My first choice was to present a chronological listing of every sensei who had studied under another sensei, eventually leading to my sensei, Seki. My second choice was to present only the sensei who had founded or altered major ryu and whose teachings made their way to my sensei. I chose the latter for two reasons. First, listing only the major sensei would result in a smoother and more functional chart that was much easier to remember. Second, it wasn't possible to get complete background information on Sanzo Seki (Jack Seki's father) and Harold Brosious (from whom I learned elements of ketsugo).

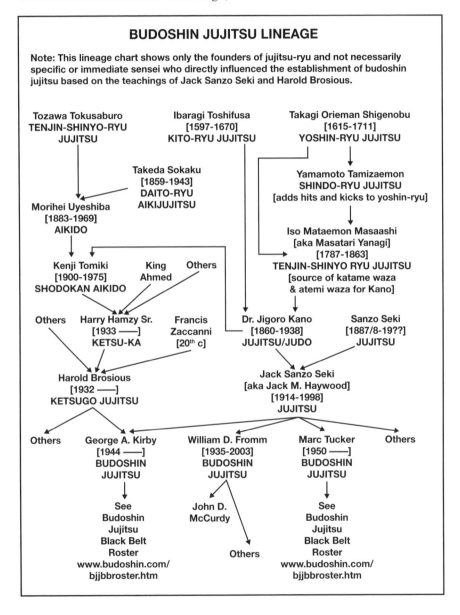

BUDOSHIN JUJITSU LINEAGE

Note: This lineage chart shows only the founders of jujitsu-ryu and not necessarily specific or immediate sensei who directly influenced the establishment of budoshin jujitsu based on the teachings of Jack Sanzo Seki and Harold Brosious.

CLOSING REMARKS

$\mathbf{B}$udoshin jujitsu preserves the concepts of *bujutsu*, *bugei* and *bunkai*. It does so because it teaches the art and applies it to street self-defense situations from the first moment the student gets on the mat as a white belt and through his entire martial arts career. Students are taught to defend themselves, which is what the art is designed for (bujutsu). Advanced students learn how to break down techniques into their separate elements and reintegrate them into different but effective self-defense applications (bunkai). Even more advanced students in the art acquire the theory behind common movements, which will help them teach the art to others (bugei).

A street-effective martial art cannot be practiced solo. This is why students of budoshin jujitsu are put into a street situation from the very outset—a situation in which they must use skills they are still learning. This helps the students react to attacks with initially specific responses. But they are learning to respond to street attacks quickly rather than being dumbfounded by the attack itself. The effective use of those skills can only be acquired with continuous practice, even if it must be simulated or limited to prevent injury, mainly to the attacker. It is fine to teach an art solely as an art, if the student understands it as such. However, the student's ability to defend himself is a skill separate from learning any martial art itself. Unless the student has the experience of successfully integrating the martial art he is learning and responding to street attacks automatically and immediately, he will be unable to defend himself, regardless of what martial art(s) he has learned.

After 30 years, I have made some changes in the way I teach. I have learned a lot about the art in the years since I wrote this book, and I'm still learning. In expanding *Jujitsu: Basic Techniques of the Gentle Art*, I expanded my own understanding of the art and its history. Seki was right in saying that we are always still white belts who are still learning the art. If you are serious about your art, you can easily spend your life learning it. But knowing it is quite another story.

Change *is* inevitable. Richard Miles, my first junior high-school principal, had a sign on the wall behind his desk that read: "The only thing permanent is change." If the methods of teaching the art can be improved on, the success rate for those learning the art will be greater. This should be every sensei's goal. At the same time, the art itself is the final product and remains untouched. The path up the same mountain can always be improved on—to a point—for any martial art. This is why a martial art is an art.

Your path for studying budoshin jujitsu should be much more complete and smoother now as compared to 30 years ago, but I also believe that it will be just as challenging.

GLOSSARY

Aikido Combination of *ai* (mind), *ki* (spirit/energy) and *do* (way). *Aikido* takes techniques involving the use of the attacker's energy and momentum from the parent art of *jujitsu* to evolve a separate system of self-defense. Aikido, founded by Morihei Uyeshiba, is considered to be one of the least violent martial arts. However, its techniques can be devastating.

Aikijitsu A style of *jujitsu* in which joint manipulation is emphasized as a means of subduing an assailant.

Ashi Foot.

Atama Head.

Budoshin Literal translation is *bu* (martial), *do* (way), *shin* (spirit).

Bugei Refining the tactics of *bujutsu* so they can be taught in an organized manner within a *dojo* environment.

Bujutsu Practical application of martial arts skills, as in street combat.

Bunkai Taking each technique apart for analysis and teaching each move or element separately.

Come-Along A hold or lock on a person, usually by applying pressure to a joint to force a person to move in a direction you desire; used in conjunction with a standing submission.

Dan Black-belt (instructor) grades, usually starting at first *dan (shodan)* and moving up to 10th dan *(judan)*.

Deflect Similar to a block except your goal is to move in the direction of the attacking limb out of the way, usually just two to four inches, without stopping or significantly reducing the momentum of the attacking extremity.

Dojo A place where a martial art is taught.

Eri Lapel.

Gari Rear sweep.

Guruma Circular (usually includes a joint lock); also *kudema*.

Hane Inside (sweep).

Harai Outside sweep. *(Ashi harai* = low sweep. *Koshi harai* = high sweep.)

Hasami Scissor.

Hiji Elbow.

Hiki Pull.

Hypogastrium Lower part of the stomach area. Metaphysical tradition holds that your *ki* is located approximately one to two inches below the navel at the hypogastrium or *saiki tanden* (lower stomach). That is where the center of your energy or center of gravity is located. It is the focal point for many *jujitsu* techniques.

Ippon One point.

Judo Combination of *ju* (gentle) and *do* (way). Dr. Jigoro Kano took many of the throws, groundwork and submissions of *jujitsu* and simplified them into what is known as judo.

Juji To cross.

Jujitsu Combination of *ju* (gentle) and *jitsu* (art). May also be spelled *jujitsu, jiujitsu, jiu-jitsu, jujutsu, ju-jutsu, jiujutsu* and *jiu-jutsu.*

Jutte Combination of *ju* (10) and *te* (hand). When put together, this martial arts weapon is referred to as the power-of-10-hands weapon. While this single-hooked truncheon was originally designed to disarm samurai, it also can be used as an extremely effective defensive weapon that inflicts severe and/or permanent injury on the assailant.

Karada Body.

Karate Combination of *kara* (empty) and *te* (hand). It may also be referred to as *karatedo* with the *do* (way). Karatedo means "of the hand way." Some styles of karate, especially *kenpo (kempo)* karate, evolved from the hits, kicks and strikes of *jujitsu* to simplify the art.

Karate Chop A misnomer; actually a *shuto* or knife-edge strike with the outside edge of the hand with fingers together and straight.

Karatejitsu Ideally, a style of *jujitsu* in which karate techniques are emphasized.

Kata A specific technique in *jujitsu*. Ideally, it would also include a distraction move or technique and a finishing technique (hold, submission, come-along, pin, strike, hit or kick).

Kao Face.

Ketsugo A style of *jujitsu*, formalized by Harold Brosious. The defense system is a blend of the various systems of jujitsu, featuring circle, spiral and acquisition techniques. As of 2011, there are two to three different systems of *ketsugo* jujitsu in the United States.

Ki Your inner spirit or energy expended in executing any movement or technique.

Kiai *Ki* (spirit) and *ai* (mind). When combined, it means "spirit meeting." When used as a shout during the execution of a technique, a *kiai* will give you extra energy/spirit to successfully execute whatever technique you are doing—plus it may actually scare/intimidate your attacker with the power you possess.

Kime-No-Kata Practicing the form of the technique without actually executing it on your training partner *(uke)*. It may also refer to prearranged forms if a series of forms is practiced without a partner.

Kinteki Groin.

Koshi/Goshi Hip. Spelled *goshi* if not used as the first word in a technique as the phonetic sound "k" changes to a "g" sound.

Kubi Neck.

Kuzushi The practice of off-balancing your opponent either physically or mentally through the use of physical and/or verbal distractions.

Kyu Belt ranks below black-belt grades. All *kyu* grades are considered "student" or sometimes even "beginner" grades. Kyu grades usually move from a higher number to a lower number; e.g., seventh to first kyu in *budoshin jujitsu*.

Loosen Up The use of one or a series of hits, nerve attacks, kicks, etc., used as a distraction to force the attacker's attention away from what you want to do or to lessen his resistance to your defensive technique. A single distraction can increase your opponent's reaction time (how long it takes him to physically react to what you have done) by .3 to .7 seconds.

Mae Forward.

Maitta "I submit!" When said, the *uke* gives up or indicates submission to a technique. Submission may be indicated by saying *maitta* (pronounced mah-tay), by tapping the mat or your partner with your hand or foot, or by tapping your head if no other extremity is available, until your partner releases his hold.

Maki To wind.

Makikomi Winding throw.

Mushin Literally interpreted as "no-mind." *Mushin* actually refers to a high skill level in any subject or matter in which no conscious effort is expended to accomplish a goal and in which the person completing such a task usually has no recall of all the specific steps he took to effectively complete the task at hand. A state of mushin is essential for any effective self-defense action.

Nage Throw.

Ogoshi Major/high.

Osoto Outside.

Otoshi Drop throw.

Ouchi Inner.

Parent Art A martial art from which other martial arts or ways evolved.

Pivot To move the designated foot backward (usually) in a large circle—left foot counterclockwise and right foot clockwise.

Proselytize To actively and aggressively advocate a specific idea, action or style of martial art to others with the intent of getting others to change their minds and follow your lead.

Ready Position Your starting position for all defensive techniques in *jujitsu* and in this book; allows you to face your opponent in a balanced position with a minimum of your body exposed to attack. Your feet should be about shoulder-width apart, with the closest foot facing the attacker and the back foot at about a 45-degree angle. This may either be a right (left shoulder forward) or left (right shoulder forward) ready position. Your hands are positioned in one of the following ways: 1) clasped one over the other (left hand over your right fist) if in the right ready position; 2) your left arm is up and ready to block and your right fist in a *gingitzu* (formal position); 3) both hands are up (open or closed in a fist) ready to block an attack; or 4) both hands are up and facing the attacker, which usually signals a desire to not fight while still maintaining an effective blocking/deflecting position.

Ryu Refers to a style of a martial art. *Ryu* may be added directly to the end of a word, hyphenated or added after the word indicating the style of the martial art. Valid examples are *goshindoryu*, *goshindo-ryu* and *goshindo ryu*.

Saiki Tanden Lower stomach, about two inches below the navel. It is considered to be the source location of a person's *ki* and center of balance.

Senaka Back (shoulder).

Sensei Teacher.

Seoi Sleeve; Sometimes misspelled *seol* with an "l" rather than an "i" because of phonetic pronunciation conflicts between Japanese and English.

Shark Bite (pinch) A pinch with the tips of the thumb and index finger, ideally using your nails only, to sensitive parts of the human body, especially inside the upper arm, sides of the torso and inside the thighs. A "shark bite" can provide quick intense pain as a distraction even if a person is insensitive to nerve attacks.

Shimi/Shime Refers to any lock, hold or choke that causes pain. In *jujitsu*, this also includes *shioku waza* (nerve techniques).

Shioku Refers to any nerve technique. All *shioku waza* are *shimi waza* but not all shimi waza are shioku waza.

Small-Circle Theory A technical theory, initially advocated by professor Wally Jay, states that efficiency of movement (smaller circles and better balance of the *tori)* results in more effective movements with less physical effort.

Standing Submission Finishing a technique with your opponent still standing, locked or held in a position in which resistance by him or a continuation of the technique by you would result in injury to the attacker. It usually involves pressure on or the locking of a bone joint (used in conjunction with a come-along).

Tai Body.

Tatake Attack.

Te Hand.

Tekubi Wrist. This is the older term for the more modern *kote*. *Tekubi* literally translates into the "neck of the hand." The technique *tekubi shimi waza* (wrist-lock takedown) also can be called *kote gaeshi* if you wish to use the more modern term.

Takedown A technique, hold, lock, etc., designed to bring the attacker down to the ground without throwing him. One or both his feet may remain on the ground. The lock, hold, etc., is maintained throughout the technique and even after the attacker is down because of a submission hold or pin.

Tatami A mat on which practice throws and other martial arts techniques are performed.

Throw A technique or hold designed to unbalance an attacker and physically lift him off his feet and cause him to hit the ground as the technique is completed.

Tomoe Circle. A *tomoe nage* may be referred to as a circle throw or a stomach throw if you throw your opponent over you by placing one foot in his lower stomach as you go down onto your back, pulling him over you, as in a circle.

Tori The person who is practicing techniques. Also referred to as the "defender."

Ube Thumb.

Ude Arm.

Uke The person who attacks the *tori* in practice; the attacker.

Ukemi Breakfall.

Ura Rear (opposite, negative).

Ushiro Back.

Waza The first meaning is "technique." The second meaning is as a self-defense term in *jujitsu;* it refers to a combination of moves in response to a street attack beginning with 1) a response to the attack, followed by 2) a follow-through (throw, takedown or standing lock) and usually ending up with 3) a hold, strike, pin, lock or come-along that can be considered a submission.

Word of Mouth Factual or nonfactual events, history or other information that is passed from one person to another, or from one generation to another verbally, rather than being written down.

Yoko Side.

Yubi Finger(s).

Yudanshakai An organization of black belts in a martial art.

Photo by Thomas Sanders

ABOUT THE AUTHOR

George Kirby, winner of *Black Belt*'s 2007 Hall of Fame Instructor of the Year Award, is a 10th-degree black belt in *jujitsu* and an internationally recognized martial arts instructor. He is the author of the popular *Jujitsu* series, and he published its first installment, *Jujitsu: Basic Techniques of the Gentle Art*, in 1983. The other titles in the series include *Jujitsu: Intermediate Techniques of the Gentle Art*, *Jujitsu Nerve Techniques: The Invisible Weapon of Self-Defense*, *Advanced Jujitsu: The Science Behind the Gentle Art* and *Jujitsu Figure-4 Locks: Submission Holds of the Gentle Art*.

Kirby has taught jujitsu since 1967 and currently teaches jujitsu for the Santa Clarita Parks and Recreation Department. In addition, he serves on the board of directors for Budoshin Ju-Jitsu Dojo and the American Ju-Jitsu Association. He is also the founder of Budoshin Ju-Jitsu Yudanshakai, an educational foundation. He continues to organize the Budoshin Ju-Jitsu Summer Camp and Camp Budoshin every year.

To learn more about *budoshin* jujitsu, visit www.budoshin.com.

BLACK BELT®
World's Leading Magazine of Martial Arts

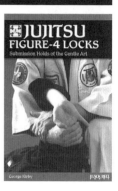

JUJITSU FIGURE-4 LOCKS
Submission Holds of the Gentle Art

George Kirby

HALL OF FAME
Search *Black Belt*'s online cache of articles for a wide variety of topics, names, styles and more!

Register Now

Find your martial arts style GO

Search

ARCHIVE FEATURE

George Kirby:
2007 Instructor of the Year   ✉ EMAIL   🖨 PRINT

George Kirby:
2007 Instructor of the Year

By Jon Sattler

For some, teaching is nothing more than a steady paycheck. For *jujutsu* master George Kirby, it's a calling that he's uniquely and undeniably suited for.

Long before the Brazilian *jiu-jitsu* revolution swept the United States, the amiable Kirby began studying the gentle art to help deal with the stress of grad school. Little did he know that his tutelage under *sensei* Jack "Sanzo" Seki was the beginning of a martial arts journey that would shape America's understanding of jujutsu for decades to come.

By 1968, Seki could sense Kirby's potential as an instructor and told him and fellow-student Bill Fromm about an opening at a local YMCA in Burbank, California. When Kirby pointed out that as brown belts they were too inexperienced to teach, Seki responded, "Now you're both black belts. Act like it."

And so began the teaching career of one of traditional jujutsu's most respected and beloved masters. A year later, Kirby followed another one of Seki's suggestions and collaborated with Fromm to form the **American Ju-Jitsu Association**. Under Kirby's stewardship, first as president and now as chairman, the AJA has grown into a governing body renowned for bringing together jujutsu practitioners from around the world. He's also the founder and chairman of the Budoshin Ju-Jitsu Dojo Inc., a nonprofit educational foundation, and the **Budoshin Ju-Jitsu Yudanshakai**, a research and educational foundation.

George Kirby
(Photo by Thomas Sanders)

Kirby's collaborations are too numerous to list in their entirety, but a few of the groups he's donated his time to helping are the Budo Centre International, Nippon Seibukan, Shorinji Ryu JuJitsu Association and World Head of Family Sokeship Council.

Despite his busy schedule as an ambassador of the arts, teaching has always been Kirby's passion. Following his sensei's advice, Kirby taught jujutsu and self-defense at the Burbank YMCA until 1974, when he received an opportunity to expand his program with the Burbank Parks and Recreation Department. His partnership with the city lasted until 1996, when he decided to take on the challenge of launching a new jujutsu program for the city of Santa Clarita, California, where he continues to share what he's learned. Along the way, he perfected his craft in the public-school system, where he taught jujutsu and social studies for nearly four decades.

Following the Rodney King controversy, Kirby worked with a handful of other nationally known martial artists to develop for the Los Angeles Police Department what would become one of the nation's best arrest-and-control training programs. In 1998 the city of Los Angeles awarded him a Certificate of Appreciation for his role as a defensive-tactics consultant on the Civilian Martial Arts Advisory Panel.
The LAPD isn't the only organization to recognize Kirby's outstanding work. The California Branch Jujitsu Federation twice awarded him the title of Outstanding Instructor, and he's earned the Amateur Athletic Union Jujitsu National Sports Award and a certificate of honor from the Federation of Practicing Jujutsuans.

His dedication to teaching extends well beyond the classroom and the dojo. A prolific writer, Kirby has penned a half-dozen **books** on jujutsu, and his essays have appeared in numerous publications, including *Black Belt*. He's also preserved his teachings digitally with an eight-part DVD study course.

In 2000 Kirby reached the pinnacle of his profession when he was promoted to *judan*, or 10-degree black belt. In recognition of his 40 years of teaching, *Black Belt* is proud to induct him into its Hall of Fame as 2007 Instructor of the Year.

INTERMEDIATE TECHNIQUES OF THE GENTLE ART
by George Kirby

JUJITSU NERVE TECHNIQUES
The Invisible Weapon of Self-Defense
by George Kirby

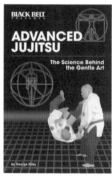

BLACK BELT
ADVANCED JUJITSU
The Science Behind the Gentle Art
by George Kirby